D1477688

# PINK FLOYD
# THE DARK SIDE OF THE MOON

## ZUM 50. JUBILÄUM

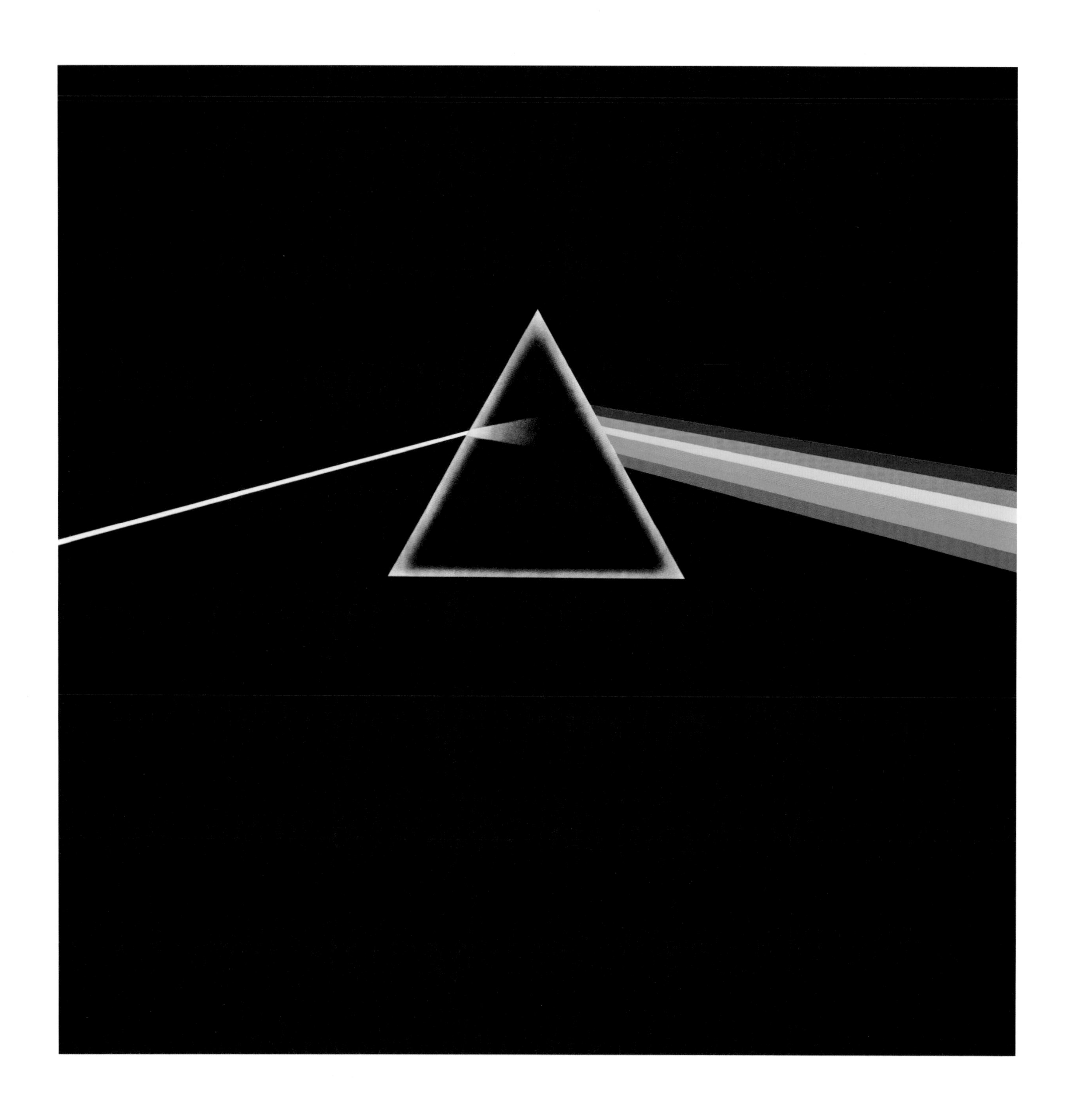

# PINK FLOYD
# THE DARK SIDE OF THE MOON

## ZUM 50. JUBILÄUM

*„There is no dark side of the moon, really.*
*Matter of fact, it's all dark.“*

Gerry O'Driscoll, Pförtner bei den Abbey Road Studios

# CAUGHT IN THE ACT

WHILE a host of current bands are injecting glamour and excitement back into rock, the Pink Floyd continue in their own way to do just the opposite. Messrs Waters, Wright, Gilmour and Mason would no sooner wear a satin jacket as finish their set with a rock medley. It's the way it should be, for the Floyd are an institution in this country and elsewhere. They are the world's number one underground band.

And while there are nowadays many who attempt to emulate their space voyage ideas, none are half as good as the Floyd in top gear. They needed no warming up at the Empire Pool,, Wembley, on Saturday. From the word go, they gave the packed stadium a faultless demonstration of what psychedelic music is all about. There wasn't a note, or a sound, out of place during the whole evening.

It's a recital more than a concert, and the Floyd don't so much give us numbers as perform pieces of music, lasting up to an hour each.

For starters on Saturday we had that lengthy work entitled "The Dark Side of the Moon", an eerie title for an equally eerie piece of music that takes the listener through a host of different moods, most of which are accompanied by unusual sounds stretching around his head by way of the group's quadraphonic sound system. I can't understand why more group's don't try this Floydian tactic: the effect is really stunning.

The second half of the recital was composed of three more major pieces, and a couple of encores. The first encore — the riveting "Set The Controls For the Heart of the Sun" — was obviously rehearsed, but the second — a bluesy jam — wasn't. It served a useful purpose to show that the group are not confined to playing science fiction soundtrack music all the time.

The incendiary gimmicks from the stage frequently obliterated the artists. Flasbombs erupted here and there at well-timed places, and Roger Waters' gong actually became a blazing sun during "Controls".

All the time the group were effectively illuminated by their imposing lighting tower at the rear of the stage which served a dual purpose — at frequent intervals it belched out smoke which mingled with the coloured lights and the dry ice surface mist to effectively wisk us all away to Planet Floyd.

Dave Gilmour is an underestimated guitarist. That he knows his instrument back to front is never really in doubt, but playing guitar with the Floyd demands an extra precision, and the ability to strike harsh chords one minute and lighter notes the next. And he has to be the handiest man around when it comes to using an echo chamber, as the extended notes proved.

Rick Wright, I suspect, contributes considerably more than just keyboards. Someone must dabble around with pre-recorded tapes and Wright seems to be the obvious choice. Both tape and keyboard work is executed with the unassuming precision that typifies the band's approach to their highly individual music.

One final thought: wouldn't it be great if, for once, they dropped the image and played "See Emily Play" — just for an encore.— CHRIS CHARLESWORTH.

PINK FLOYD: world's number one underground band

# Floyd's space odyssey

JOHN SMITH ENTERTAINMENTS
BY ARRANGEMENT WITH STEVE O'ROURKE PRESENT

# PINK FLOYD
## ON TOUR

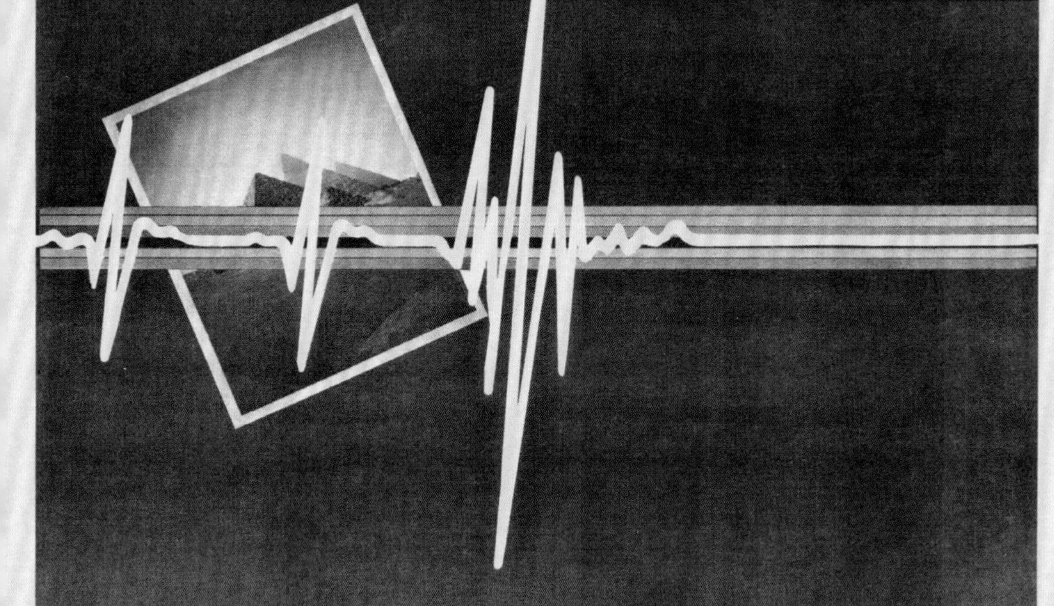

|  |  |
|---|---|
| November 4th 1974 | Usher Hall, Edinburgh. |
| 5th | |
| November 8th 1974 | Odeon, Newcastle-upon-Tyne. |
| 9th | |
| November 14th 1974 | Empire Pool, Wembley. |
| 15th | |
| 16th | |
| November 19th 1974 | Trentham Gardens, Stoke-on-Trent |
| November 22nd 1974 | Sophia Gardens, Cardiff. |
| November 28th 1974 | Empire Theatre, Liverpool. |
| 29th | |
| 30th | |
| December 3rd 1974 | Hippodrome, Birmingham. |
| 4th | |
| 5th | |
| December 9th 1974 | Palace Theatre, Manchester. |
| 10th | |
| December 13th 1974 | Hippodrome, Bristol. |
| 14th | |

All concerts are at 7.30 in the evening except Wembley – Wembley evening concerts are at 8.00

Extra Date: November 17th Empire Pool, Wembley, 6 p.m.

TICKETS ACCEPTED BY MAIL ORDER ONLY UNTIL 7th OCTOBER
LIMITED TO FOUR TICKETS PER PERSON.

SEND STAMPED ADDRESSED ENVELOPE TOGETHER WITH POSTAL ORDER TO PINK FLOYD CONCERT AT THEATRE BOX OFFICES.

ENGLANDTOUR 1972

20. JANUAR
The Dome, *Brighton*

21. JANUAR
Guildhall, *Portsmouth*

22. JANUAR
Winter Gardens, *Bournemouth*

23. JANUAR
Guildhall, *Southampton*

27. JANUAR
City Hall, *Newcastle-Upon-Tyne*

28. JANUAR
City Hall, *Leeds*

3. FEBRUAR
Locarno Ballroom, *Coventry*

5. FEBRUAR
Colston Hall, *Bristol*

10. FEBRUAR
De Montfort Hall, *Leicester*

12. FEBRUAR
City Hall, *Sheffield*

13. FEBRUAR
Empire Theatre, *Liverpool*

17.–20. FEBRUAR
Rainbow Theatre, *London*

JAPANTOUR 1972

6./7. MÄRZ
Tokyo-To Taiikukan, *Shibuya*

8./9. MÄRZ
Festival Hall, *Osaka*

10. MÄRZ
Dai-Sho-Gun Furitsu Taiikukan, *Kioto*

13. MÄRZ
Nakanoshima Sports Centre, *Sapporo*

ENGLAND 1972

29./30. MÄRZ
Free Trade Hall, *Manchester*

NORDAMERIKATOUR 1972

14. APRIL
Fort Homer W. Hesterly Armory, *Tampa*

15. APRIL
Hollywood Sportatorium, *Pembroke Pines*

16. APRIL
Township Auditorium, *Columbia*

18. APRIL
Atlanta Symphony Hall, *Atlanta*

20. APRIL
Syria Mosque Theater, *Pittsburgh*

21. APRIL
Lyric Theater, *Baltimore*

22. APRIL
Civic Theatre, *Akron*

23. APRIL
Music Hall, *Cincinnati*

24. APRIL
Allen Theatre, *Cleveland*

26./27. APRIL
Ford Auditorium, *Detroit*

28. APRIL
Auditorium Theatre, *Chicago*

29. APRIL
Spectrum Theater, *Philadelphia*

1./2. MAI
Carnegie Hall, *New York*

3. MAI
John F. Kennedy Center for Performing Arts, *Washington*

4. MAI
Music Hall, *Boston*

EUROPA 1972

18. MAI
Deutschlandhalle, *Westberlin*

ENGLAND 1972

28./29. JUNI
The Dome, *Brighton*

NORDAMERIKATOUR 1972

8. SEPTEMBER
Municipal Auditorium, *Austin*

9. SEPTEMBER
Music Hall, *Houston*

10. SEPTEMBER
Mcfarlin Auditorium, *Dallas*

11. SEPTEMBER
Memorial Hall, *Kansas City*

12. SEPTEMBER
Civic Center Music Hall, *Oklahoma City*

13. SEPTEMBER
Henry Levitt Arena, *Wichita*

15. SEPTEMBER
Community Center Arena, *Tucson*

16. SEPTEMBER
Golden Hall, *San Diego*

17. SEPTEMBER
Big Surf, *Tempe*

19. SEPTEMBER
University of Denver Arena, *Denver*

22. SEPTEMBER
Hollywood Bowl, *Los Angeles*

23./24. SEPTEMBER
Winterland Auditorium, *San Francisco*

27. SEPTEMBER
Garden Auditorium, *Vancouver*

28. SEPTEMBER
Memorial Coliseum, *Portland*

29. SEPTEMBER
Hec Edmunson Pavilion, *Seattle*

30. SEPTEMBER
Garden Auditorium, *Vancouver*

ENGLAND 1972

21. OKTOBER
Wembley Empire Pool, *London*

EUROPATOUR 1972

10./11. NOVEMBER
Kb Hallen, *Kopenhagen*

12. NOVEMBER
Ernst-Merck-Halle, *Hamburg*

14. NOVEMBER
Philipshalle, *Düsseldorf*

15. NOVEMBER
Sporthalle, *Böblingen*

16./17. NOVEMBER
Festhalle, *Frankfurt*

28. NOVEMBER
Palais des Sports, *Toulouse*

29. NOVEMBER
Parc des Expositions, *Poitiers*

1./2. DEZEMBER
Centre Sportif de L'Île des Vannes, *Paris*

3. DEZEMBER
Parc des Expositions, *Caen*

5. DEZEMBER
Vorst Nationaal, *Brüssel*

7. DEZEMBER
Palais des Sports, *Lille*

8. DEZEMBER
Parc des Expositions, *Nancy*

9. DEZEMBER
Hallenstadion, *Zürich*

10. DEZEMBER
Palais des Sports, *Lyon*

NORDAMERIKATOUR 1973

4. MÄRZ
Dane County Memorial Coliseum, *Madison*

5. MÄRZ
Cobo Arena, *Detroit*

6. MÄRZ
Kiel Opera House, *St. Louis*

7. MÄRZ
International Amphitheatre, *Chicago*

8. MÄRZ
Armory Fieldhouse, *Cincinnati*

10. MÄRZ
Memorial Gymnasium, *Kent*

11. MÄRZ
Maple Leaf Gardens, *Toronto*

12. MÄRZ
Forum de Montréal, *Montreal*

14. MÄRZ
Music Hall, *Boston*

15. MÄRZ
Spectrum Theater, *Philadelphia*

17. MÄRZ
Radio City Music Hall, *New York*

18. MÄRZ
Palace Theater, *Waterbury*

19. MÄRZ
Providence Civic Center, *Providence*

22. MÄRZ
Hampton Coliseum, *Hampton*

23. MÄRZ
Charlotte Park Center, *Charlotte*

24. MÄRZ
Municipal Auditorium, *Atlanta*

ENGLAND 1973

18./19. MAI
Earls Court, *London*

NORDAMERIKATOUR 1973

17. JUNI
Saratoga Performing Arts Center, *Saratoga*

18. JUNI
Roosevelt Stadium, *Jersey City*

19. JUNI
Civic Center Arena, *Pittsburgh*

20./21. JUNI
Merriweather Post Pavilion, *Columbia*

22. JUNI
Buffalo Memorial Auditorium, *Buffalo*

23. JUNI
Olympia Stadium, *Detroit*

24. JUNI
Blossom Music Center, *Cuyahoga*

25. JUNI
Convention Center, *Louisville*

27. JUNI
Jacksonville Coliseum, *Jacksonville*

28. JUNI
Hollywood Sportatorium,
*Pembroke Pines*

29. JUNI
Tampa Stadium, *Tampa*

EUROPA 1973

12. OKTOBER
Olympiahalle, *München*

13. OKTOBER
Stadthalle, *Wien*

ENGLAND 1973

4. NOVEMBER, 17 UHR & 21 UHR
Rainbow Theatre, *London*

FRANKREICHTOUR 1974

18. JUNI
Palais des Expositions, *Toulouse*

19. JUNI
Parc des Expositions, *Poitiers*

21. JUNI
Parc des Expositions, *Dijon*

22. JUNI
Théâtre de Plein Air, Parc des Expositions,
*Colmar*

24.–26. JUNI
Palais des Sports, *Paris*

WINTERTOURNEE GROSSBRITANNIEN 1974

4./5. NOVEMBER
Usher Hall, *Edinburgh*

8./9. NOVEMBER
Odeon, *Newcastle-Upon-Tyne*

14.–17. NOVEMBER
Wembley Empire Pool, *London*

19. NOVEMBER
Trentham Gardens, *Stoke-On-Trent*

22. NOVEMBER
Sophia Gardens Pavillion, *Cardiff*

28.–30. NOVEMBER
Empire Theatre, *Liverpool*

3.–5. DEZEMBER
The Hippodrome, *Birmingham*

9.–10. DEZEMBER
The Palace Theatre, *Manchester*

13./14. DEZEMBER
The Hippodrome, *Bristol*

NORDAMERIKATOUR 1975

8. APRIL
Pacific National Exhibition Coliseum,
*Vancouver*

10. APRIL
Seattle Center Coliseum, *Seattle*

12./13. APRIL
Cow Palace, *San Francisco*

17. APRIL
Denver Coliseum, *Denver*

19. APRIL
Tucson Community Center, *Tucson*

20. APRIL
University Activity Center, *Tempe*

21. APRIL
Sports Arena, *San Diego*

22.–27. APRIL
Los Angeles Memorial Sports Arena,
*Los Angeles*

7. JUNI
Atlanta Stadium, *Atlanta*

10. JUNI
Capital Center, *Landover*

12./13. JUNI
Spectrum Theater, *Philadelphia*

14. JUNI
Roosevelt Stadium, *Jersey City*

16./17. JUNI
Nassau Veterans Memorial Coliseum,
*Uniondale*

18. JUNI
Boston Garden, *Boston*

20. JUNI
Three Rivers Stadium, *Pittsburgh*

22. JUNI
County Stadium, *Milwaukee*

23./24. JUNI
Olympia Stadium, *Detroit*

26. JUNI
Autostade, *Montreal*

28. JUNI
Ivor Wynne Stadium, *Hamilton*

ENGLAND 1975

5. JULI
Knebworth Park, *Stevenage*

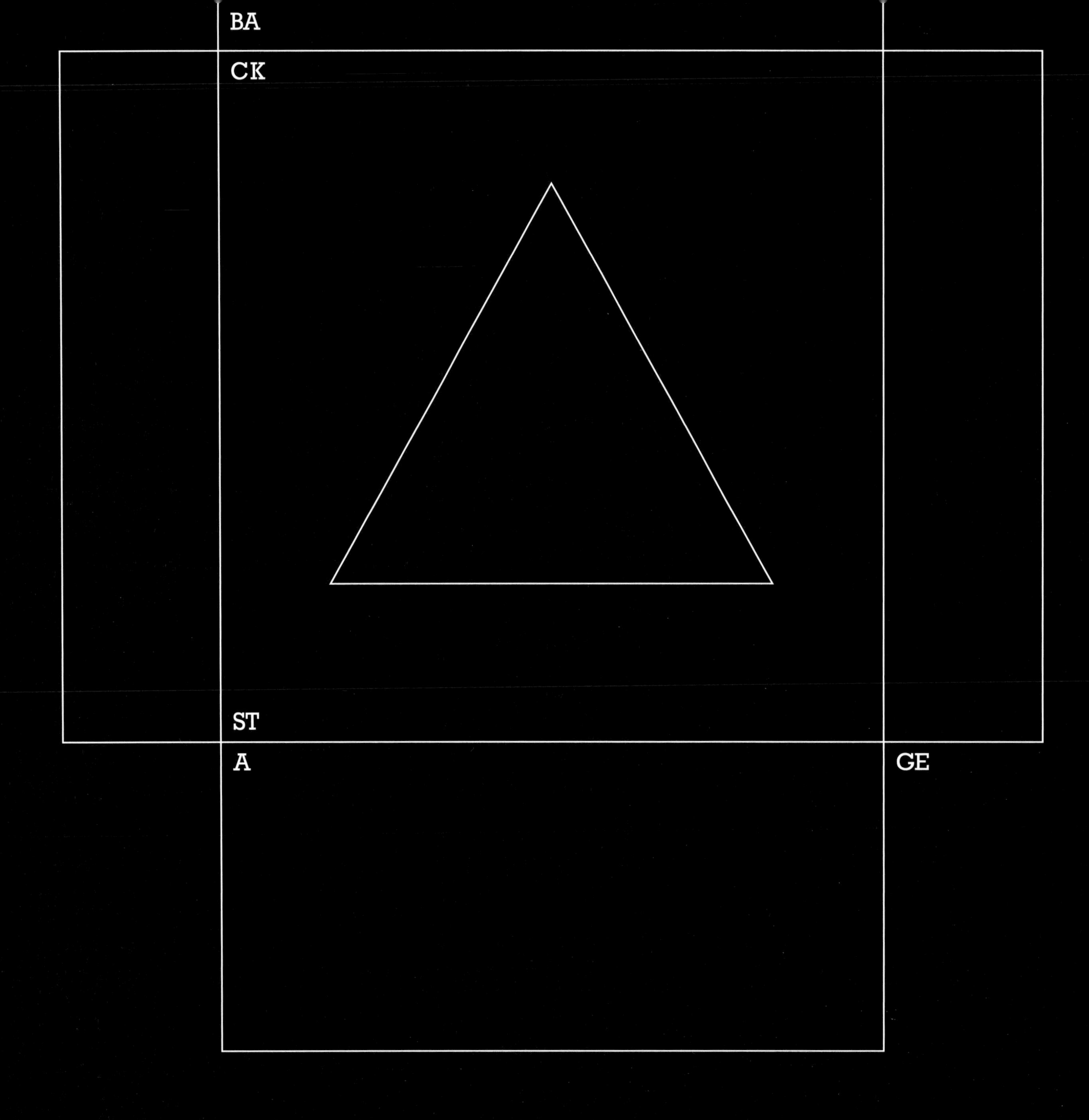
BA
CK
ST
A
GE

Heineken
5262
MATEUS

EXTRA STOUT
IN LONDON ENGLAND

BAD COMPANY

JURGENSENS

GUINNESS

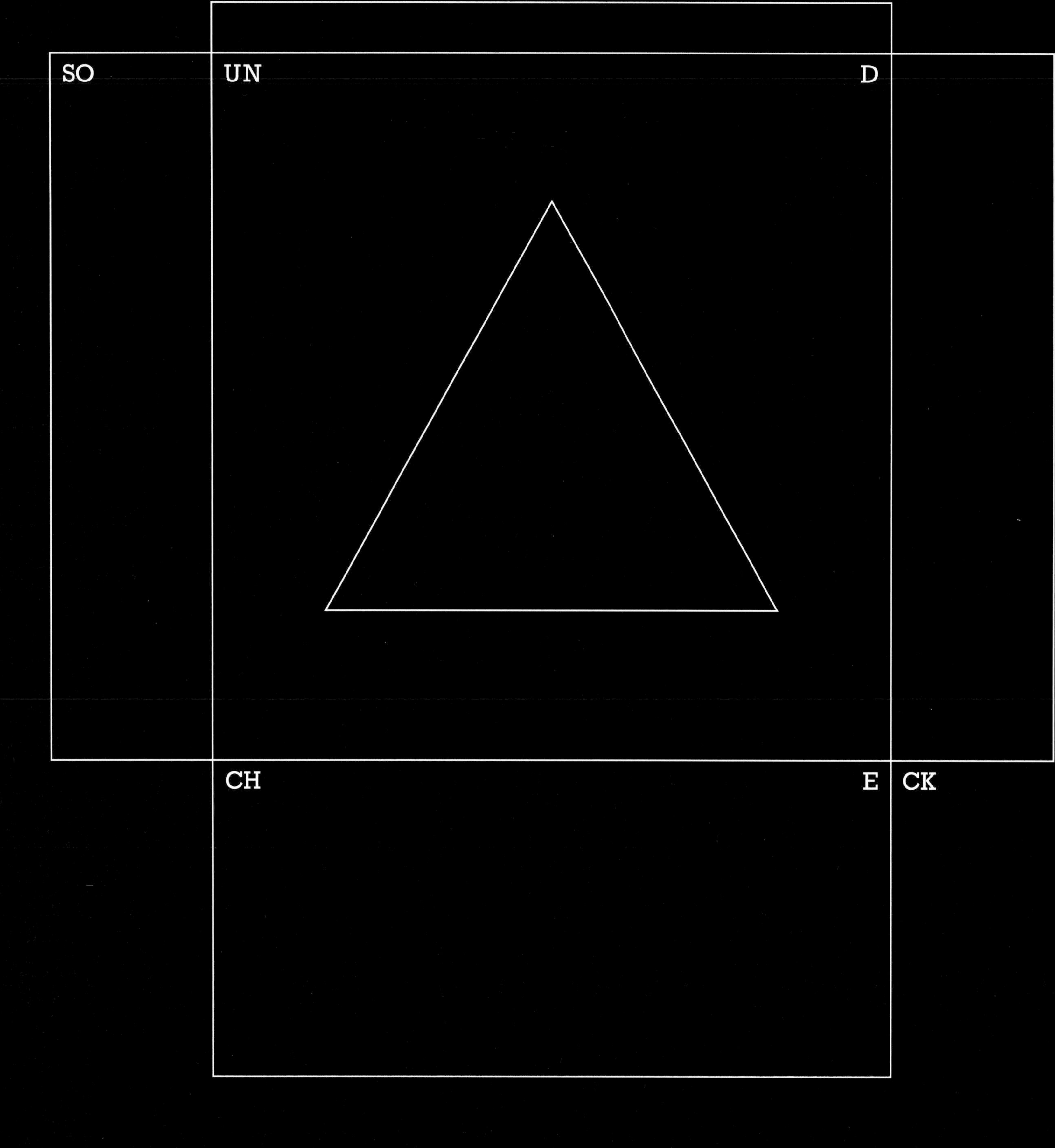
SO
UN
D
CH
E
CK

PINK 20
FLOYD

7

NEW YORK

SH

OW

S

HIWATT

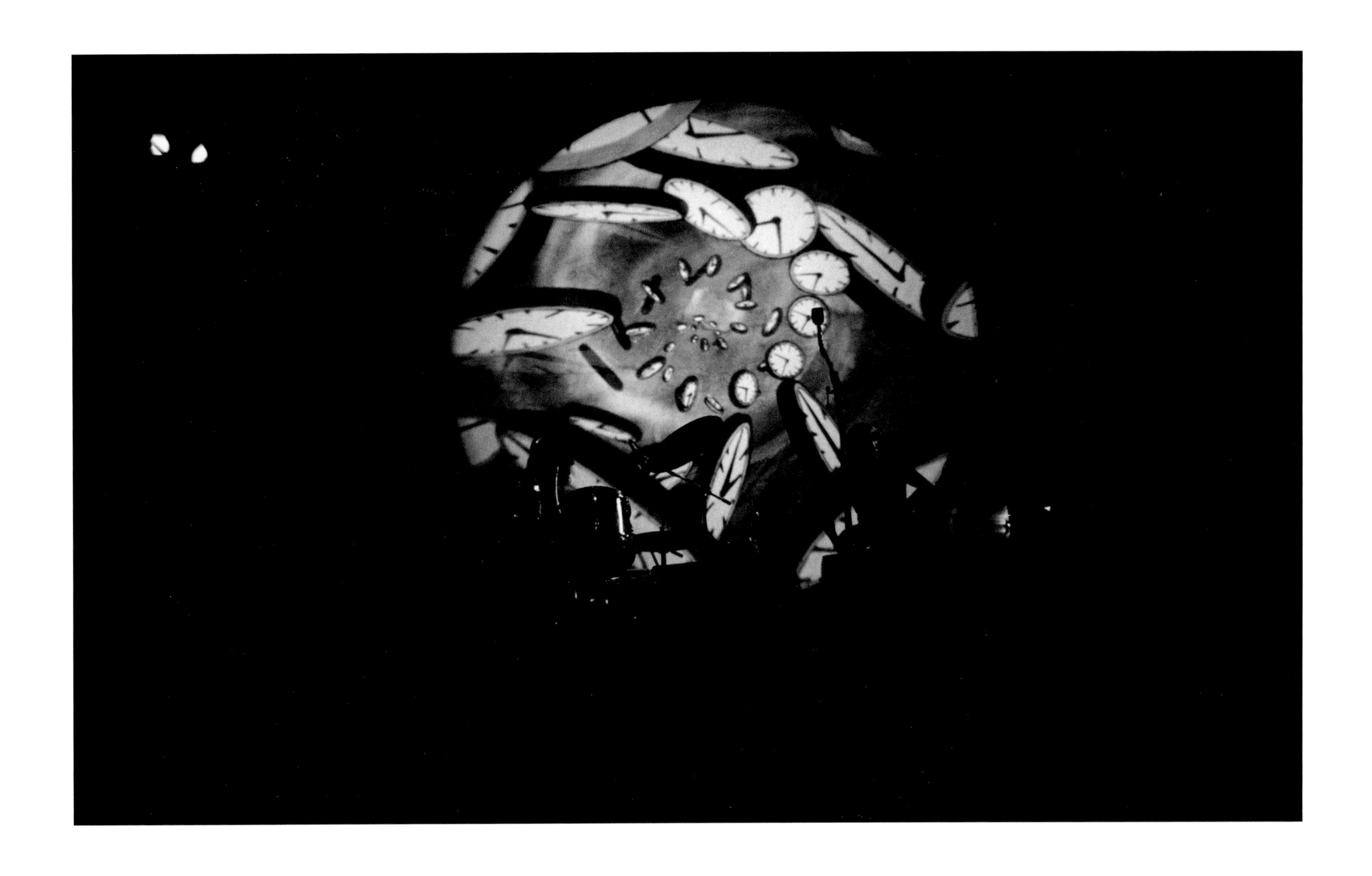

EXTRA STOUT
GUINNES

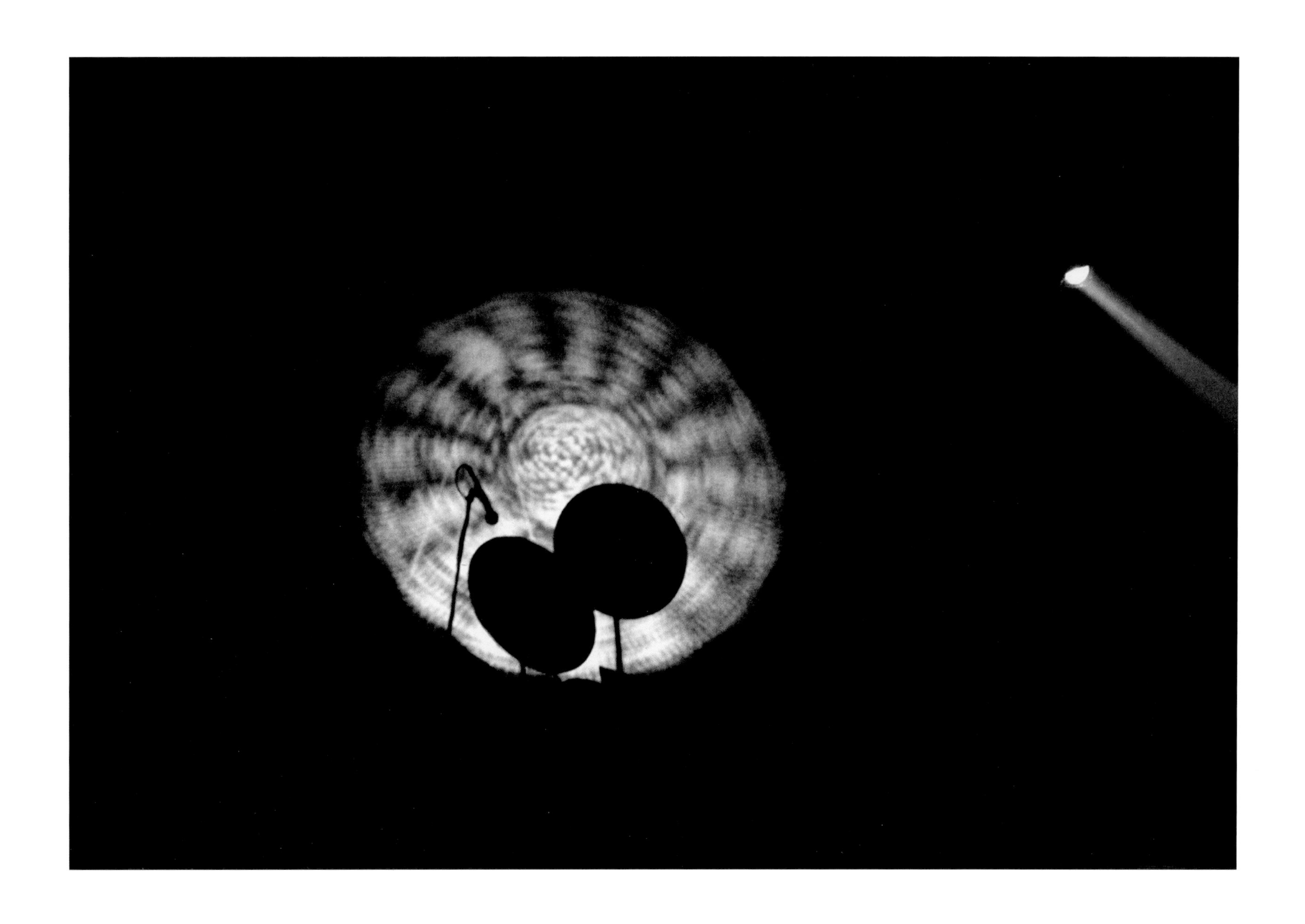

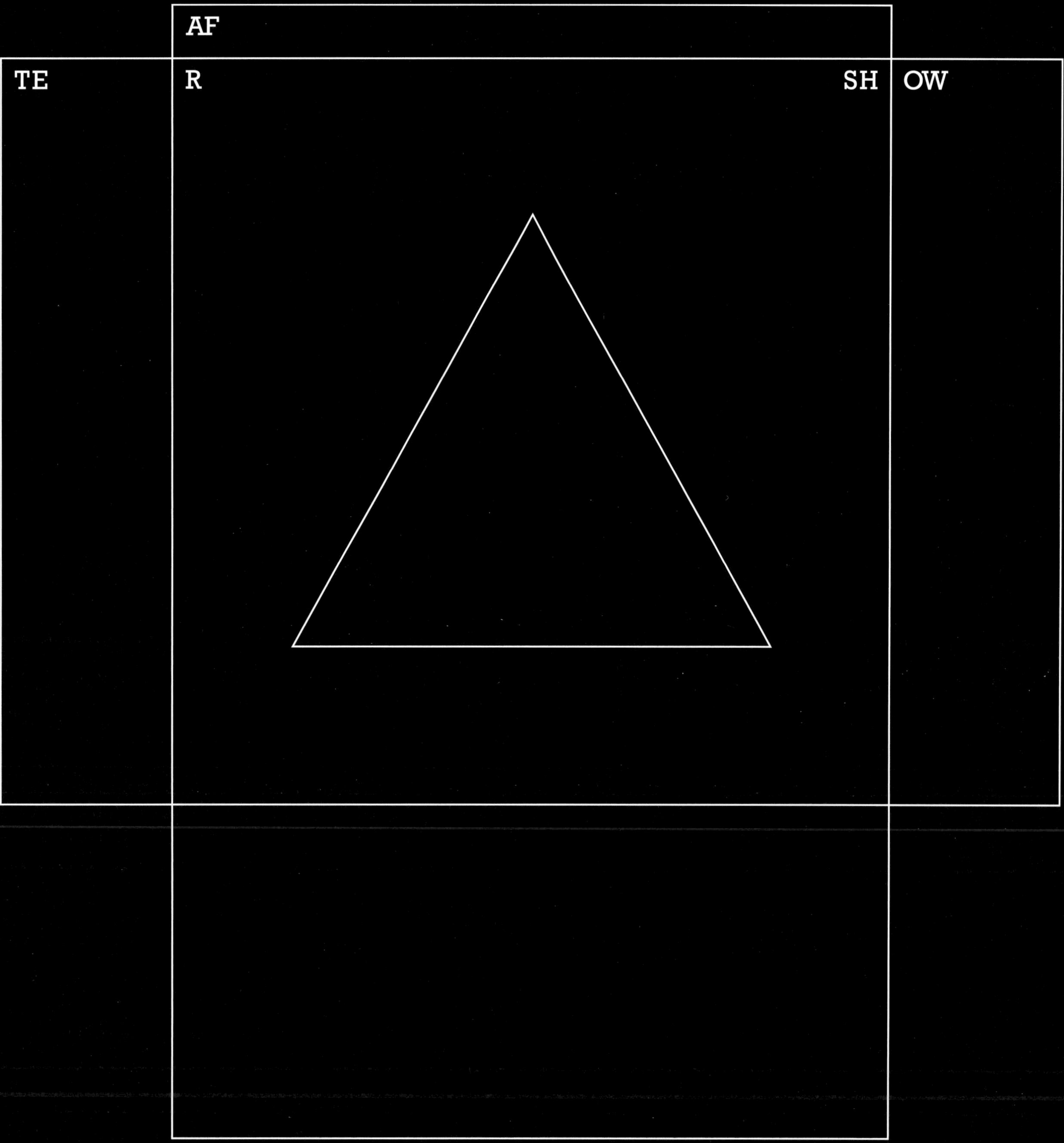
AF
TE
R
SH
OW

RENTAL FORMS TO BE
HOW TO
COMPLETE
RENTAL CARD

75,000 DEFENCE JOBS TO BE AXED
WILSON'S

PLEASE LIFT
OFF
TEMPORARY

ONION
BAGGER

ONION
BAGGER

17
18

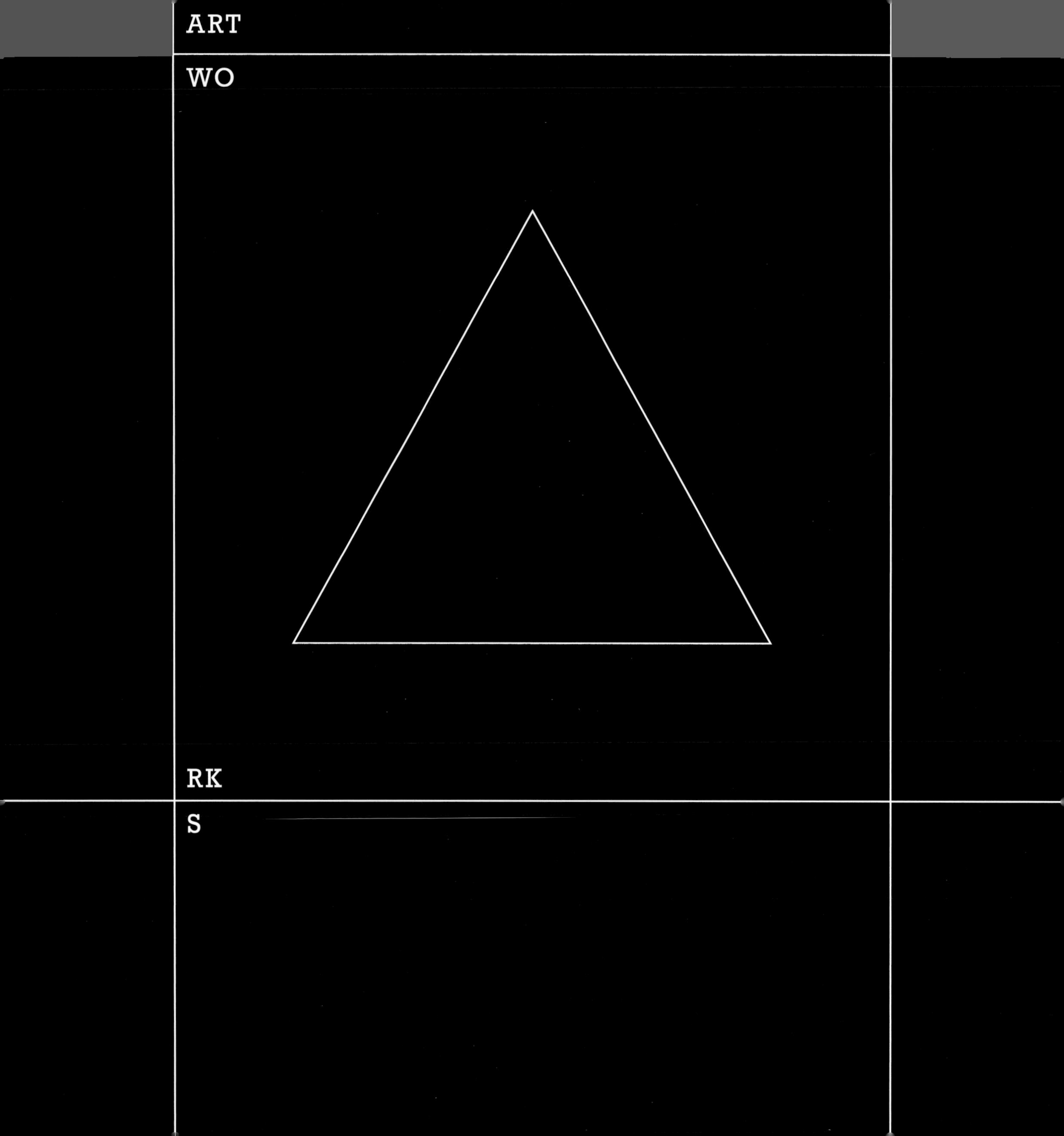
ART
WO
RK
S

THE GRAMOPHONE CO. LTD. ALL RIGHTS OF THE MANUFACTURER AND OF THE OWNER OF THE RECORDED WORK RESERVED.
EMI
Harvest
PINK FLOYD
SIDE 1
℗ 1973
The Gramophone
Company Limited
STEREO
SHVL 804
(SHVL 804A) 33⅓
THE DARK SIDE OF THE MOON
(a) (i) SPEAK TO ME (Mason)
(ii) BREATHE IN THE AIR (WATERS—Gilmour—Wright)
(b) ON THE RUN (WATERS—Gilmour)
(c) TIME (Waters—Mason—Gilmour—Wright)
(d) THE GREAT GIG IN THE SKY (Wright)
World Copyrights Ltd.
Lyrics by Roger Waters
Music by Pink Floyd
Produced by Pink Floyd
MADE IN GT. BRITAIN
UNAUTHORISED PUBLIC PERFORMANCE BROADCASTING AND COPYING OF THIS RECORD PROHIBITED.
THE GRAMOPHONE CO. LTD. ALL RIGHTS OF THE MANUFACTURER AND OF THE OWNER OF THE RECORDED WORK RESERVED.
EMI
Harvest
PINK FLOYD
SIDE 2
℗ 1973
The Gramophone
Company Limited
STEREO
SHVL 804
(SHVL 804B) 33⅓
THE DARK SIDE OF THE MOON
(e) MONEY (Waters)
(f) US AND THEM (WATERS—Wright)
(g) ANY COLOUR YOU LIKE (GILMOUR—Mason—Wright)
(h) BRAIN DAMAGE (Waters)
(i) ECLIPSE (Waters)
World Copyrights Ltd.
Lyrics by Roger Waters
Music by Pink Floyd
Produced by Pink Floyd
MADE IN GT. BRITAIN
UNAUTHORISED PUBLIC PERFORMANCE BROADCASTING AND COPYING OF THIS RECORD PROHIBITED.

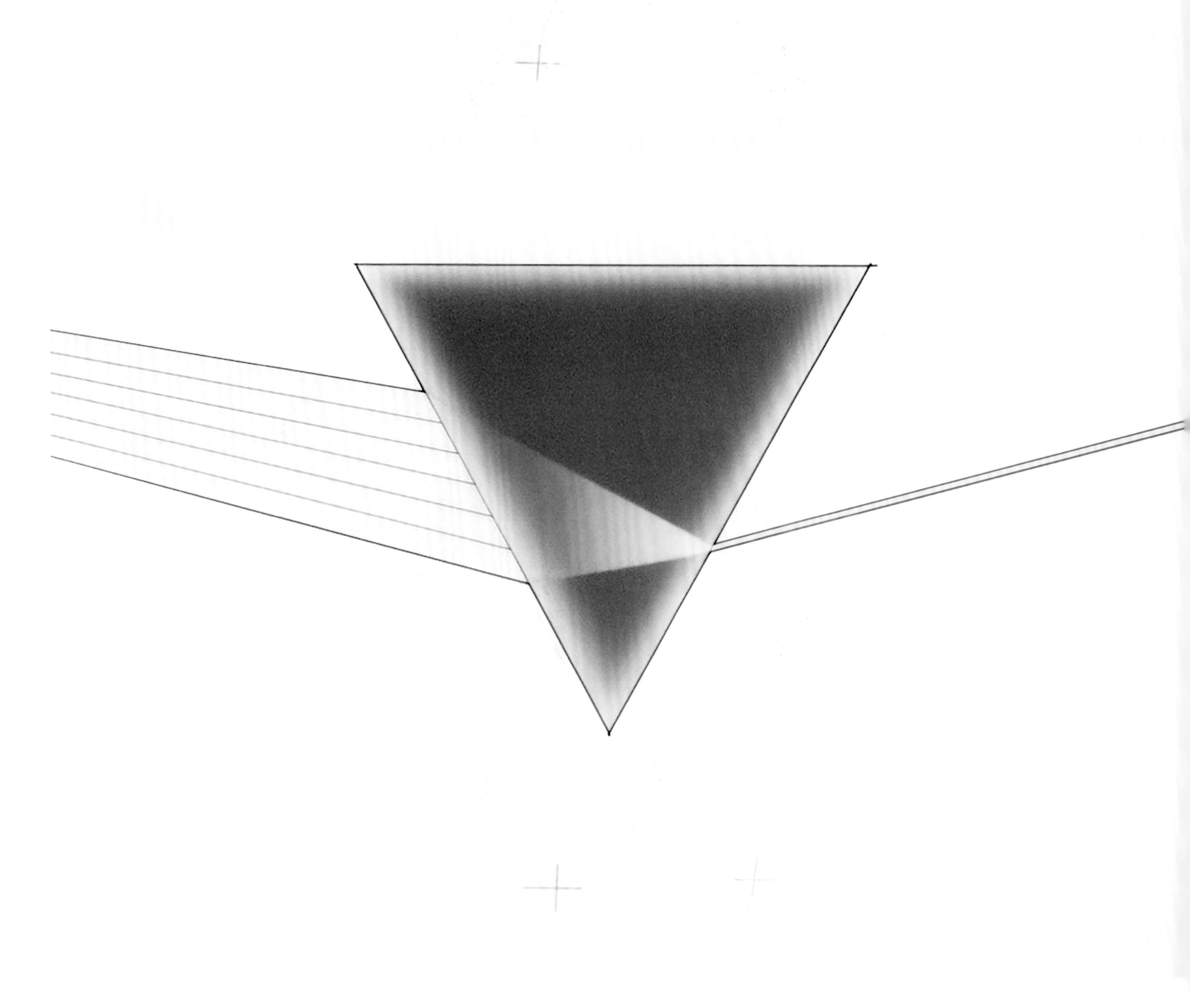

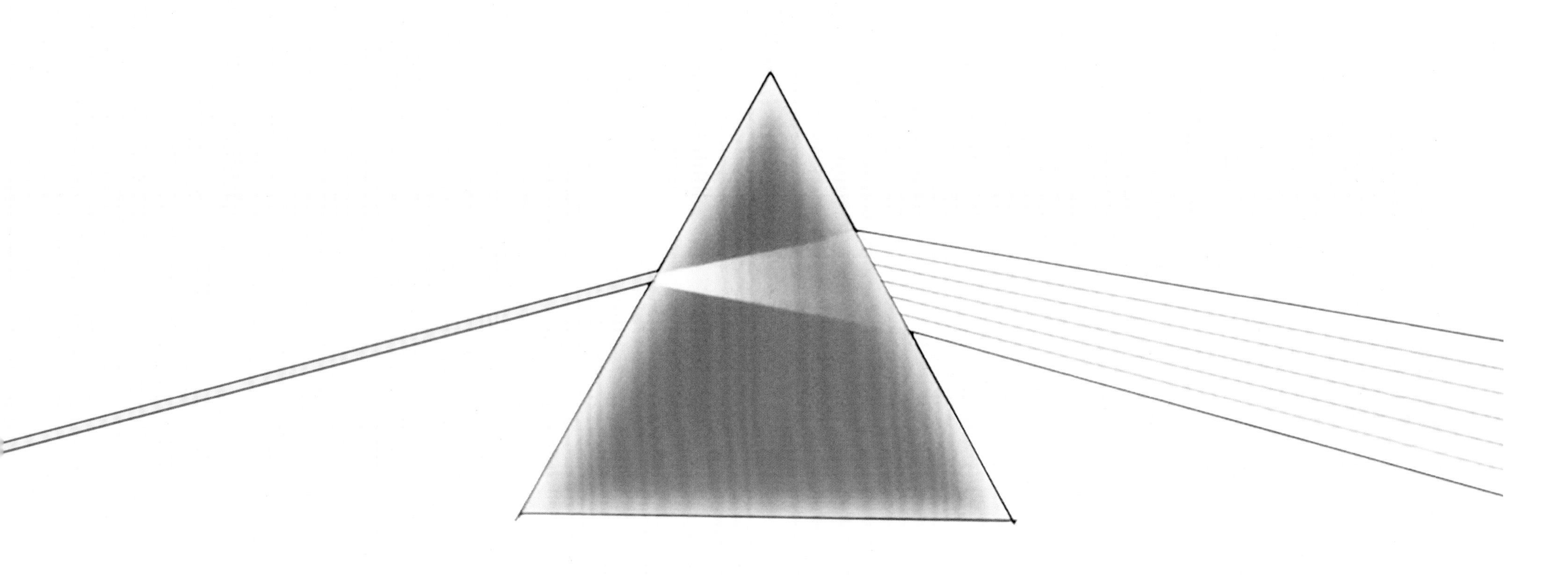

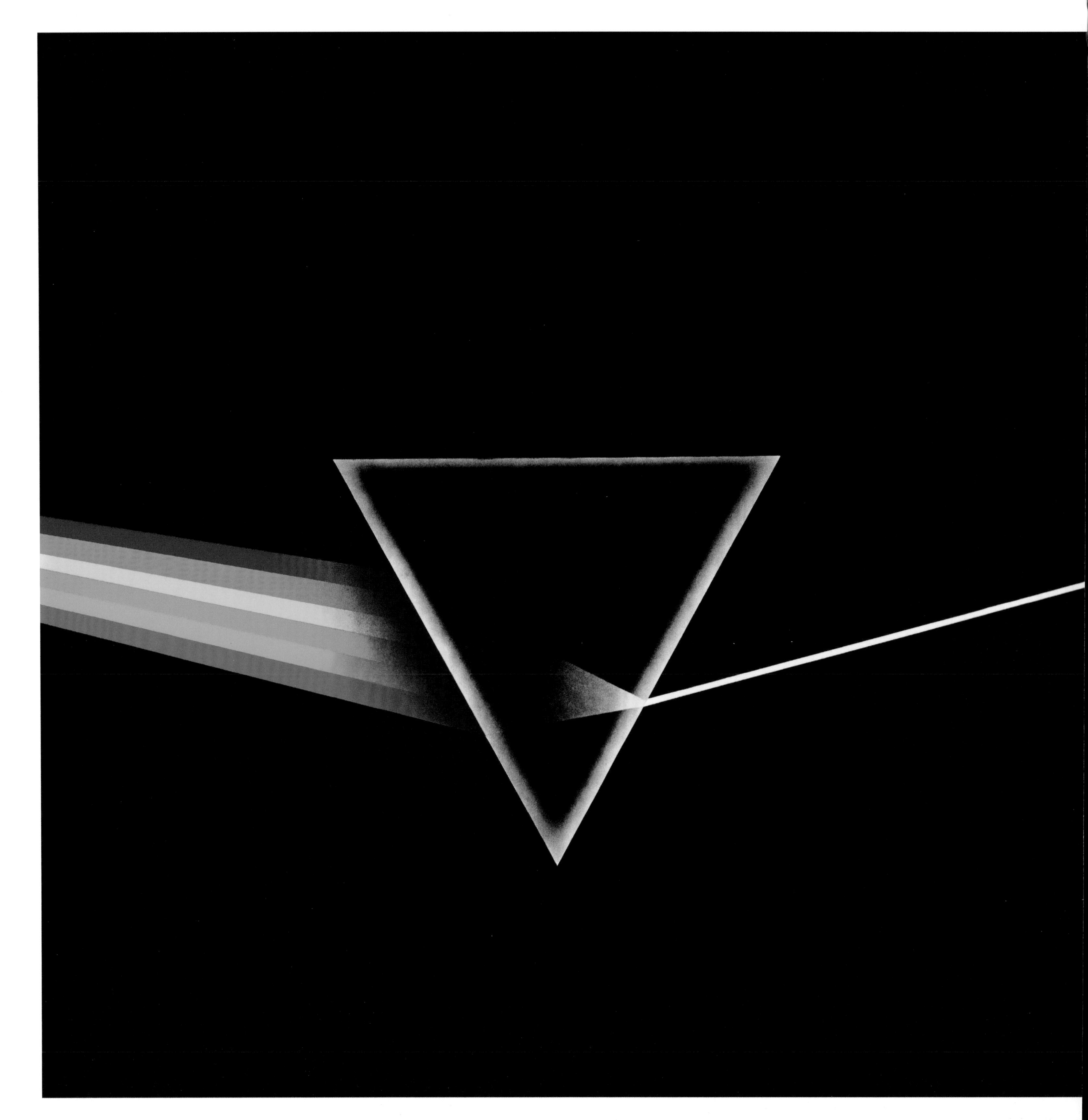

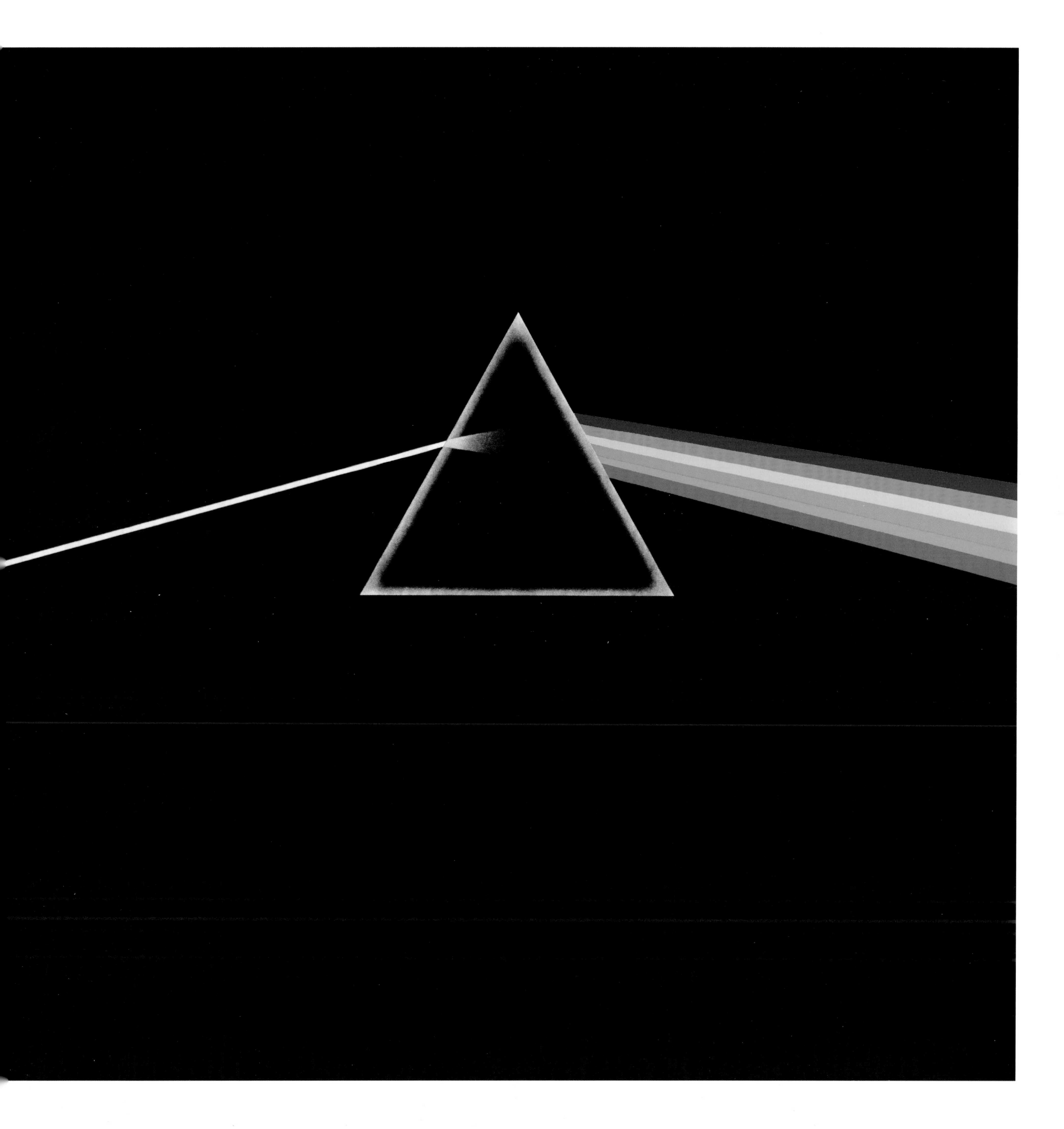

PINK FLOYD

INSIDE COVER

ALL BACKGROUND UP TO KEYLINES TO PRINT SOLID BLACK. BLACK + 80% CYAN

DROP IN SIX COLOUR TINTS AS SHOWN ON THIS OVERLAY.

* NO KEYLINES TO APPEAR

USE THE SAME SIX COLOUR TINTS FOR FRONT & BACK COVER.

SIDE ONE
1 SPEAK TO ME (Mason)
2 BREATHE (Waters, Gilmour, Wright)
3 ON THE RUN (Gilmour, Waters)
4 TIME (Mason, Waters, Wright, Gilmour)
5 THE GREAT GIG IN THE SKY (Wright)

SIDE TWO
1 MONEY (Waters)
2 US AND THEM (Waters, Wright)
3 ANY COLOUR YOU LIKE (Gilmour, Mason, Wright)
4 BRAIN DAMAGE (Waters)
5 ECLIPSE (waters)

DAVID GILMOUR Vocals, Guitars, VCS3
NICK MASON Percussion, Tape Effects
RICHARD WRIGHT Keyboards, Vocals, VCS3
ROGER WATERS Bass Guitar, Vocals, VCS3, Tape Effects

**BREATHE**

Breathe, breathe in the air
Don't be afraid to care
Leave, don't leave me
Walk around and choose your own ground
Long you live and high you fly
Smiles you'll give and tears you'll cry
All you touch and all you see
Is all your life will ever be

Run, rabbit, run
Dig that hole, forget the sun
And when at last the work is done
Don't sit down it's time to dig another one
For long you'll live, and high you'll fly
But only if you ride the tide
And balanced on the biggest wave
You race towards an early grave.

**TIME**

Ticking away the moments that make up a dull day
Fritter and waste the hours in an offhand way
Kicking around on a piece of ground in your hometown
Waiting for someone or something to show you the way

Tired of lying in the sunshine, staying home to watch the rain
You are young and life is long, and there is time to kill today
And then one day you find ten years have got behind you
No one told you when to run, you missed the starting gun

And you run, and you run to catch up with the sun but it's sinking
Racing around to come up behind you again
The sun is the same in a relative way but you're older
Shorter of breath and one day closer to death

Every year is getting shorter, never seem to find the time
Plans that either come to naught or half a page of scribbled lines
Hanging on in quiet desperation is the English way
The time is gone, the song is over, thought I'd something more to say

**Breathe Reprise**

Home, home again
I like to be here when I can
And when I come home cold and tired
It's good to warm my bones beside the fire
Far away across the field
The tolling of the iron bell
Calls the faithful to their knees
To hear the softly spoken magic spells.

**MONEY**

Money, Get away
Get a good job with more pay and you're O.K.
Money, it's a gas
Grab that cash with both hands and make a stash
New car, caviar, four star daydream
Think I'll buy me a football team

Money, get back
I'm alright Jack, keep your hands off of my stack
Money, it's a hit
Don't give me that do goody good bullshit
I'm in the hi-fidelity first class traveling set
And I think I need a Lear jet

Money, it's a crime
Share it fairly, but don't take a slice of my pie
Money, so they say
Is the root of all evil today
But if you ask for a rise it's no surprise that they're
giving none away

Produced by PINK FLOYD
Recorded at Abbey Road Studios, London
between June 1972 and January 1973

Engineer Alan Parsons
Assistant Peter James
Mixing Supervised by Chris Thomas

Saxophone on 'Us and Them' and 'Money' by Dick Parry

Vocals on 'The Great Gig in the Sky' by Clare Torry
Backing Vocals Doris Troy,
Leslie Duncan, Liza Strike, Barry St John

Sleeve Design by Hipgnosis
Sleeve Art by George Hardie N.T.A.
Photography buy Hipgnosis
Stickers Art by George Hardie N.T.A.

All lyrics by ROGER WATERS



REVERSE ALL CREDITS,
TRACK LIST & LYRICS TO
WHITE OUT OF SOLID BLACK

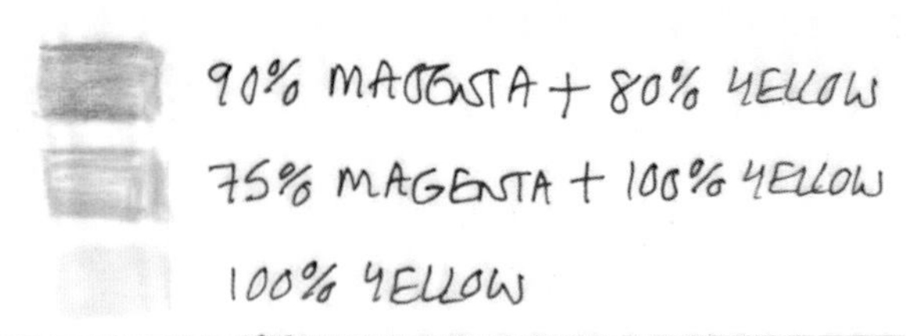


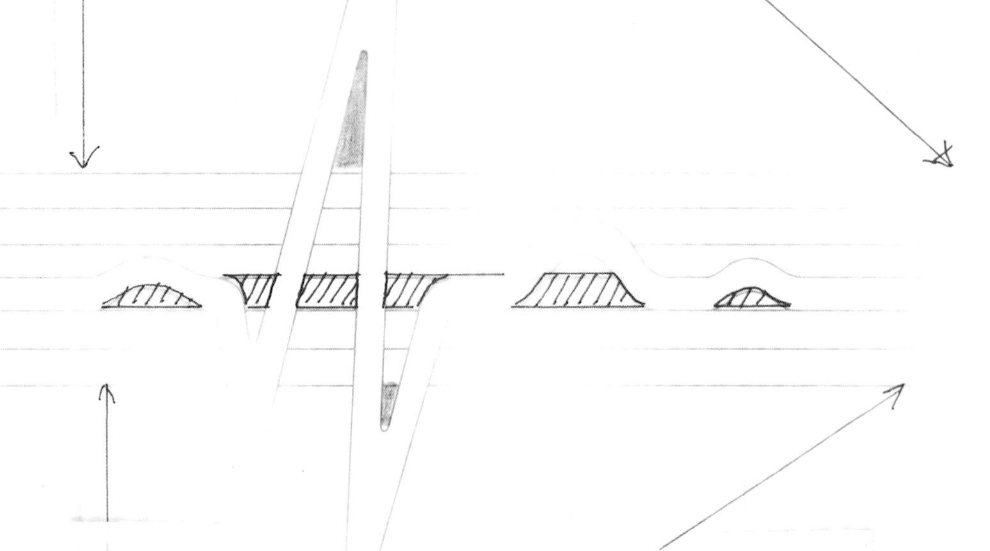

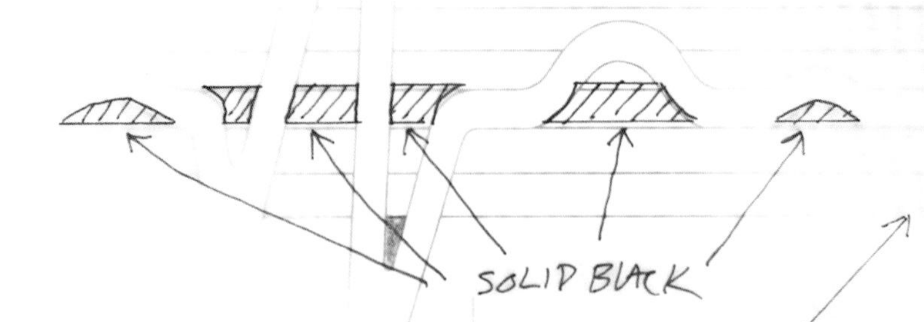


**US AND THEM**

Us, and them
And after all we're only ordinary men
Me, and you
God only knows
It's not what we would choose to do
Forward he cried from the rear
And the front rank died
And the General sat, and the lines on the map
moved from side to side
Black and blue
And who knows which is which and who is who
Up and Down
And in the end it's only round and round and round
Haven't you heard it's a battle of words
the poster bearer cried
Listen son, said the man with the gun
There's room for you inside

Down and Out
It can't be helped but there's a lot of it about
With, without
And who'll deny it's what the fighting's all about
Out of the way, it's a busy day
I've got things on my mind
For the want of the price of tea and a slice
The old man died

**BRAIN DAMAGE**

The lunatic is on the grass
The lunatic is on the grass
Remembering games and daisy chains and laughs
Got to keep the loonies on the path

The lunatic is in the hall
The lunatics are in my hall
The paper holds their folded faces to the floor
And every day the paper boy brings more

And if the dam breaks open many years too soon
And if there is no room upon the hill
And if your head explodes with dark forebodings too
I'll see you on the dark side of the moon

The lunatic is in my head
The lunatic is in my head
You raise the blade, you make the change
You re-arrange me 'til I'm sane

You lock the door
And throw away the key
There's someone in my head but it's not me.

And if the cloud bursts, thunder in your ear
You shout and no one seems to hear
And if the band you're in starts playing different tunes
I'll see you on the dark side of the moon

**ECLIPSE**

All that you touch
And all that you see
All that you taste
All you feel
And all that you love
And all that you hate
All you distrust
All you save
All that you give
All that you deal
All that you buy
beg, borrow or steal
All you create
All you destroy
All that you do
All that you say
All that you eat
everyone you meet
All that you slight
everyone you fight
All that is now
All that is gone
All that's to come
and everything under the sun is in tune
but the sun is eclipsed by the moon.

SIDE ONE
1 SPEAK TO ME (Mason)
2 BREATHE (Waters, Gilmour, Wright)
3 ON THE RUN (Gilmour, Waters)
4 TIME (Mason, Waters, Wright, Gilmour)
5 THE GREAT GIG IN THE SKY (Wright)

SIDE TWO
1 MONEY (Waters)
2 US AND THEM (Waters, Wright)
3 ANY COLOUR YOU LIKE (Gilmour, Mason, Wright)
4 BRAIN DAMAGE (Waters)
5 ECLIPSE (Waters)

DAVID GILMOUR Vocals, Guitars, VCS3
NICK MASON Percussion, Tape Effects
RICHARD WRIGHT Keyboards, Vocals, VCS3
ROGER WATERS Bass Guitar, Vocals, VCS3, Tape Effects

**BREATHE**

Breathe, breathe in the air
Don't be afraid to care
Leave but don't leave me
Look around and choose your own ground
For long you live and high you fly
And smiles you'll give and tears you'll cry
And all you touch and all you see
Is all your life will ever be

Run rabbit run
Dig that hole, forget the sun,
And when at last the work is done
Don't sit down it's time to start another one
For long you live and high you fly
But only if you ride the tide
And balanced on the biggest wave
You race toward an early grave.

**TIME**

Ticking away the moments that make up a dull day
You fritter and waste the hours in an off hand way
Kicking around on a piece of ground in your home town
Waiting for someone or something to show you the way

Tired of lying in the sunshine staying home to watch the rain
You are young and life is long and there is time to kill today
And then one day you find ten years have got behind you
No one told you when to run, you missed the starting gun

And you run and you run to catch up with the sun, but it's sinking
And racing around to come up behind you again
The sun is the same in the relative way, but you're older
Shorter of breath and one day closer to death

Every year is getting shorter, never seem to find the time
Plans that either come to naught or half a page of scribbled lines
Hanging on in quiet desperation is the English way
The time is gone the song is over, thought I'd something more to say

**Breathe Reprise**

Home, home again
I like to be here when I can
When I come home cold and tired
It's good to warm my bones beside the fire
Far away across the field
The tolling of the iron bell
Calls the faithful to their knees
To hear the softly spoken magic spells.

**MONEY**

Money, get away
Get a good job with more pay and your O.K.
Money it's a gas
Grab that cash with both hands and make a stash
New car, caviar, four star daydream,
Think I'll buy me a football team

Money get back
I'm all right Jack keep your hands of my stack.
Money it's a hit
Don't give me that do goody good bullshit
I'm in the hi-fidelity first class travelling set
And I think I need a Lear jet

Money it's a crime
Share it fairly but don't take a slice of my pie
Money so they say
Is the root of all evil today
But if you ask for a rise it's no surprise that they're
giving none away


EMI

E.M.I RECORDS (The Gramophone Company Ltd)
HAYES · MIDDLESEX · ENGLAND


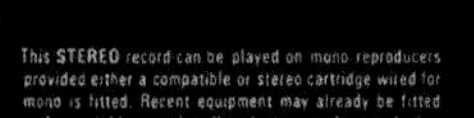
This STEREO record can be played on mono reproducers provided either a compatible or stereo cartridge wired for mono is fitted. Recent equipment may already be fitted with a suitable cartridge. If in doubt consult your dealer.

Made and printed in the EU
File under POPULAR : Pop Groups
L 7303 TPS
SHVL 804

Produced by PINK FLOYD
Recorded at Abbey Road Studios, London
between June 1972 and January 1973

Engineer Alan Parsons
Assistant Peter James
Mixing Supervised by Chris Thomas

Saxophone on 'Us and Them' and 'Money' Dick Parry

Vocals on 'The Great Gig in the Sky' by Clare Torry
Backing Vocals Doris Troy,
Leslie Duncan, Liza Strike, Barry St John

Sleeve Design by Hipgnosis
Sleeve Art by George Hardie N.T.A.
Photography by Hipgnosis
Stickers Art by George Hardie N.T.A.

All lyrics by ROGER WATERS.



**US AND THEM**

Us, and them
And after all we're only ordinary men
Me, and you
God only knows it's not what we would choose to do
Forward he cried from the rear
and the front rank died
And the General sat, and the lines on the map
moved from side to side
Black and blue
And who knows which is which and who is who
Up and Down
And in the end it's only round and round and round
Haven't you heard it's a battle of words
the poster bearer cried
Listen son, said the man with the gun
There's room for you inside

Down and Out
It can't be helped but there's a lot of it about
With, without
And who'll deny it's what the fighting's all about
Out of the way, it's a busy day
I've got things on my mind
For want of the price of tea and a slice
The old man died

**BRAIN DAMAGE**

The lunatic is on the grass
The lunatic is on the grass
Remembering games and daisy chains and laughs
Got to keep the loonies on the path

The lunatic is in the hall
The lunatics are in my hall
The paper holds their folded faces to the floor
And every day the paper boy brings more

And if the dam breaks open many years too soon
And if there is no room upon the hill
And if your head explodes with dark forbodings too
I'll see you on the dark side of the moon

The lunatic is in my head
The lunatic is in my head
You raise the blade, you make the change
You re-arrange me 'till I'm sane

You lock the door
And throw away the key
There's someone in my head but it's not me.

And if the cloud bursts, thunder in your ear
You shout and no one seems to hear
And if the band you're in starts playing different tunes
I'll see you on the dark side of the moon.

**ECLIPSE**

All that you touch
All that you see
All that you taste
All you feel
All that you love
All that you hate
All you distrust
All you save
All that you give
All that you deal
All that you buy
beg, borrow or steal
All you create
All you destroy
All that you do
All that you say
All that you eat
everyone you meet
All that you slight
everyone you fight
All that is now
All that is gone
All that's to come
and everything under the sun is in tune
but the sun is eclipsed by the moon.

02 ALBUMCOVER 1973
*Hipgnosis/George Hardie*

04 PINK FLOYD 1971 *Richard Wright, David Gilmour, Nick Mason* und *Roger Waters* im Belsize Park, London, UK.
*Pink Floyd Music Ltd*

05 PINK FLOYD 1971 *Richard Wright, Roger Waters, Nick Mason* und *David Gilmour* im Belsize Park, London, UK.
*Pink Floyd Music Ltd*

06 ZEITUNGSAUSSCHNITT 1972 Chris Charlesworths Kritik des Konzerts im Wembley Empire Pool, London, UK, erschienen in *Melody Maker*, 28. Oktober 1972.
*Pink Floyd Archive*

07 OKTOBER 1974 Anzeige im *New Musical Express* mit den Tourdaten der Englandtour für November und Dezember 1974.
*Pink Floyd Archive*

BACKSTAGE

11 JUNI 1972 *Richard Wright, Nick Mason, Roger Waters* und *David Gilmour* backstage im Dome in Brighton (UK).
*Jill Furmanovsky Archive*

12 JUNI 1972 *Richard Wright, Nick Mason* und PA-Sounddesigner *Bill Kelsey* backstage im Dome in Brighton (UK).
*Jill Furmanovsky Archive*

13 JUNI 1972 *Roger Waters* und *David Gilmour* backstage im Dome in Brighton (UK).
*Jill Furmanovsky Archive*

14 NOVEMBER 1974 *Nick Mason* in einem „Lucky Shifts"-T-Shirt, backstage in der Usher Hall in Edinburgh (UK).
*Jill Furmanovsky Archive*

15 APRIL 1975 *Roger Waters* backstage in der Los Angeles Memorial Sports Arena (USA).
*Storm Thorgerson und Aubrey „Po" Powell, Hipgnosis, Pink Floyd Music Ltd*

16 NOVEMBER 1974 *David Gilmour* backstage in der Usher Hall, Edinburgh (UK).
*Jill Furmanovsky Archive*

17 DEZEMBER 1974 Hipgnosis-Albumdesigner *Aubrey „Po" Powell* fotografiert *Richard Wright*, backstage im Hippodrome in Birmingham (UK).
*Storm Thorgerson und Aubrey „Po" Powell, Hipgnosis, Pink Floyd Music Ltd*

18 NOVEMBER 1974 Saxofonist *Dick Parry* und Fotograf *Peter Christopherson* backstage im Empire Theatre, Liverpool (UK).
*Storm Thorgerson und Aubrey „Po" Powell, Hipgnosis, Pink Floyd Music Ltd*

19 NOVEMBER 1974 *Nick Mason* beim Betrachten von Farbdias mit der Rockfotografin *Jill Furmanovsky* backstage im Empire Theatre, Liverpool (UK).
*Storm Thorgerson und Aubrey „Po" Powell, Hipgnosis, Pink Floyd Music Ltd*

20 NOVEMBER 1974 *Nick Mason* und Begleitsängerin *Carlena Williams* backstage im Empire Theatre in Liverpool (UK).
*Storm Thorgerson und Aubrey „Po" Powell, Hipgnosis, Pink Floyd Music Ltd*

21 APRIL 1975 *Roger Waters* und Begleitsängerin *Venetta Fields* backstage in der Los Angeles Memorial Sports Arena (USA).
*Storm Thorgerson und Aubrey „Po" Powell, Hipgnosis, Pink Floyd Music Ltd*

22 DEZEMBER 1974 Die Sängerinnen *Carlena Williams* und *Venetta Fields* backstage im Palace Theatre, Manchester (UK).
*Storm Thorgerson und Aubrey „Po" Powell, Hipgnosis, Pink Floyd Music Ltd*

23 APRIL 1975 *Nick Mason* mit zwei jungen Mitgliedern der Tourcrew in der Los Angeles Memorial Sports Arena (USA).
*Storm Thorgerson und Aubrey „Po" Powell, Hipgnosis, Pink Floyd Music Ltd*

24 APRIL 1975 *Storm Thorgerson* von Hipgnosis backstage in der Los Angeles Memorial Sports Arena (USA).
*Storm Thorgerson und Aubrey „Po" Powell, Hipgnosis, Pink Floyd Music Ltd*

25 DEZEMBER 1974 *Roger Waters, David Gilmour* und Hipgnosis-Designer *Aubrey „Po" Powell* backstage im Hippodrome, Birmingham (UK).
*Jill Furmanovsky Archive*

26 DEZEMBER 1974 *Nick Mason, Roger Waters, Richard Wright, David Gilmour* und Pink-Floyd-Freund *Nick Sedgwick* backstage im Hippodrome, Birmingham (UK).
*Storm Thorgerson und Aubrey „Po" Powell, Hipgnosis, Pink Floyd Music Ltd*

27 NOVEMBER 1974 *David Gilmour, Roger Waters, Richard Wright, Nick Mason* und Begleitsängerin *Carlena Williams* lesen den *Melody Maker* (Schlagzeile: „Bad Company geht ab!"), backstage im Empire Theatre in Liverpool (UK).
*Storm Thorgerson und Aubrey „Po" Powell, Hipgnosis, Pink Floyd Music Ltd*

28 NOVEMBER 1974 *David Gilmour* und *Roger Waters* spielen Backgammon, *Richard Wright* schaut zu, Bandkumpel *Nick Sedgwick* nicht, backstage in der Usher Hall, Edinburgh (UK).
*Storm Thorgerson und Aubrey „Po" Powell, Hipgnosis, Pink Floyd Music Ltd*

29 APRIL 1975 *Roger Waters* und *David Gilmour* backstage in der Los Angeles Memorial Sports Arena (USA).
*Storm Thorgerson und Aubrey „Po" Powell, Hipgnosis, Pink Floyd Music Ltd*

30 APRIL 1975 *David Gilmour, Richard Wright, Roger Waters* und Pink-Floyd-Freund *Nick Sedgwick* backstage im Pacific Coliseum, Vancouver (Kanada).
*Storm Thorgerson und Aubrey „Po" Powell, Hipgnosis, Pink Floyd Music Ltd*

31 NOVEMBER 1974 *Roger Waters* und *Richard Wright* backstage im Empire Theatre, Liverpool (UK).
*Storm Thorgerson und Aubrey „Po" Powell, Hipgnosis, Pink Floyd Music Ltd*

32 NOVEMBER 1974 *Richard Wright* und seine damalige Frau *Juliette Gale* backstage im Empire Theatre, Liverpool (UK).
*Storm Thorgerson und Aubrey „Po" Powell, Hipgnosis, Pink Floyd Music Ltd*

33 NOVEMBER 1974 *Nick Mason* und *David Gilmour* backstage im Empire Theatre, Liverpool (UK).
*Storm Thorgerson und Aubrey „Po" Powell, Hipgnosis, Pink Floyd Music Ltd*

34 NOVEMBER 1974 *David Gilmour* und *Richard Wright* backstage im Empire Theatre, Liverpool (UK).
*Storm Thorgerson und Aubrey „Po" Powell, Hipgnosis, Pink Floyd Music Ltd*

35 NOVEMBER 1974 *Nick Mason* spielt den US-Komiker *Jimmy Durante*, Bandfreund *Nick Sedgwick* sitzt dabei, backstage in der Usher Hall, Edinburgh (UK).
*Storm Thorgerson und Aubrey „Po" Powell, Hipgnosis, Pink Floyd Music Ltd*

36 APRIL 1975 *David Gilmour* stimmt seine Gitarre, backstage im Pacific Coliseum, Vancouver (Kanada).
*Storm Thorgerson und Aubrey „Po" Powell, Hipgnosis, Pink Floyd Music Ltd*

37 NOVEMBER 1974 *Roger Waters* und Bandmanager *Steve O'Rourke* backstage im Wembley Empire Pool, London (UK).
*Storm Thorgerson und Aubrey „Po" Powell, Hipgnosis, Pink Floyd Music Ltd*

SOUNDCHECK

39 APRIL 1975 Ein Roadie mit einem Block Trockeneis zur Erzeugung von Nebeleffekten auf der Bühne, backstage in der Los Angeles Memorial Sports Arena (USA).
*Storm Thorgerson und Aubrey „Po" Powell, Hipgnosis, Pink Floyd Music Ltd*

40 APRIL 1975 Ein Bühnenarbeiter ruht sich aus, backstage im University Activity Centre in Arizona (USA).
*Storm Thorgerson und Aubrey „Po" Powell, Hipgnosis, Pink Floyd Music Ltd*

41 APRIL 1975 *Pete Revell, Graeme Fleming* und andere Roadies mit dem Modellflugzeug, das während der Show über das Publikum flog und mit einer

spektakulären Explosion auf die Bühne stürzte, Tucson Community Center, Arizona (USA).
*Storm Thorgerson und Aubrey „Po" Powell, Hipgnosis, Pink Floyd Music Ltd*

42 DEZEMBER 1974 Die Roadcrew beim Aufbau der Bühnenleinwand im Hippodrome, Bristol (UK).
*Storm Thorgerson und Aubrey „Po" Powell, Hipgnosis, Pink Floyd Music Ltd*

43 APRIL 1975 Sicherheitsleute in der Los Angeles Memorial Sports Arena (USA).
*Storm Thorgerson und Aubrey „Po" Powell, Hipgnosis, Pink Floyd Music Ltd*

44 NOVEMBER 1974 *Nick Mason, David Gilmour* und Roadie *Bernie Caulder* beim Soundcheck in der Usher Hall, Edinburgh (UK).
*Jill Furmanovsky Archive*

45 NOVEMBER 1974 *David Gilmour* und Hipgnosis-Albumgestalter *Storm Thorgerson* beim Soundcheck in der Usher Hall, Edinburgh (UK).
*Jill Furmanovsky Archive*

46 NOVEMBER 1974 *Roger Waters, Nick Mason* und Lichtdesigner *Arthur Max* beim Soundcheck am Mischpult im Wembley Empire Pool, London (UK).
*Jill Furmanovsky Archive*

47 NOVEMBER 1974 *Richard Wright* und Lichtdesigner *Arthur Max* am Mischpult beim Soundcheck im Wembley Empire Pool, London (UK).
*Jill Furmanovsky Archive*

48 NOVEMBER 1974 *David Gilmour* und der leitende Gitarrentechniker *Phil Taylor* beim Soundcheck im Wembley Empire Pool, London (UK).
*Jill Furmanovsky Archive*

49 NOVEMBER 1974 *Roger Waters, Nick Mason* und *Richard Wright* beim Soundcheck auf der Bühne des Empire Theatre, Liverpool (UK).
*Storm Thorgerson und Aubrey „Po" Powell, Hipgnosis, Pink Floyd Music Ltd*

50 DEZEMBER 1974 *David Gilmour* und *Roger Waters* beim Soundcheck im Hippodrome, Birmingham (UK).
*Jill Furmanovsky Archive*

51 DEZEMBER 1974 *Nick Mason, David Gilmour* und *Roger Waters*, Soundcheck auf der Bühne des Hippodrome, Birmingham (UK).
*Jill Furmanovsky Archive*

52 APRIL 1975 *Roger Waters*, Produktionsleiter *Robbie Williams*, Toningenieur *Brian Humphries* und PA-Techniker *Bill Kelsey* beim Soundcheck im Pacific Coliseum, Vancouver (Kanada).
*Storm Thorgerson und Aubrey „Po" Powell, Hipgnosis, Pink Floyd Music Ltd*

53 NOVEMBER 1974 Begleitsängerin *Venetta Fields* liest beim Soundcheck in der Usher Hall in Edinburgh (UK) das „Floyd"-Comicprogramm.
*Jill Furmanovsky Archive*

54 APRIL 1975 Bühnensoundcheck in der Los Angeles Memorial Sports Arena (USA)
*Storm Thorgerson und Aubrey „Po" Powell, Hipgnosis, Pink Floyd Music Ltd*

55 NOVEMBER 1974 Bühnensoundcheck in der Usher Hall in Edinburgh (UK).
*Jill Furmanovsky Archive*

56 DEZEMBER 1974 Die Tourcrew, vorne: *Paul Devine, Pete Revell, Bernie Caulder, Paul Murray*, Tonbandtechniker *Mick Kluczynski*, (unbekannt), Gitarrencheftechniker *Phil Taylor*, (unbekannt); hinten: *Graeme Fleming, Coon Thompson*, Produktionsleiter *Robbie Williams*, (unbekannt), *Nick Rochford, Mick Marshall* und Unbekannte im Palace Theatre, Manchester (UK).
*Pink Floyd Archive*

57 APRIL 1975 Pink-Floyd-Fans vor dem Konzert im Pacific Coliseum, Vancouver (Kanada).
*Storm Thorgerson und Aubrey „Po" Powell, Hipgnosis, Pink Floyd Music Ltd*

SHOWS

59 APRIL 1975 Pink-Floyd-Fans in der Los Angeles Memorial Sports Arena (USA).
*Storm Thorgerson und Aubrey „Po" Powell, Hipgnosis, Pink Floyd Music Ltd*

60 JUNI 1972 *Roger Waters* beim Konzert im Dome in Brighton (UK).
*Jill Furmanovsky Archive*

61 JUNI 1972 *David Gilmour, Nick Mason* und *Roger Waters* auf der Bühne des Dome in Brighton (UK).
*Jill Furmanovsky Archive*

62 APRIL 1975 Die Band mit Lightshow und Trockeneisnebel auf der Bühne des Pacific Coliseum in Vancouver (Kanada).
*Storm Thorgerson und Aubrey „Po" Powell, Hipgnosis, Pink Floyd Music Ltd*

63 MAI 1973 Pink Floyd in Trockeneisnebeln im Londoner Earls Court (UK).
*Jill Furmanovsky Archive*

64 OKTOBER 1972 Die Band, umrahmt von Lightshow und Trockeneisnebel im Wembley Empire Pool, London (UK).
*Jill Furmanovsky Archive*

65 NOVEMBER 1974 Pink-Floyd-Fans im Wembley Empire Pool in London (UK).
*Jill Furmanovsky Archive*

66 MAI 1973 Pink Floyd live im Earls Court, London (UK).
*Jill Furmanovsky Archive*

67 NOVEMBER 1974 *David Gilmour* mit seiner Jedson-Elektro-Steelgitarre im Empire Theatre in Liverpool (UK).
*Jill Furmanovsky Archive*

68 NOVEMBER 1973 *Roger Waters* auf der Bühne des Rainbow Theatre in London (UK).
*Jill Furmanovsky Archive*

69 NOVEMBER 1973 Die Begleitsängerinnen *Vicki Brown, Liza Strike* und *Clare Torry* beim Auftritt im Rainbow Theatre, London (UK).
*Jill Furmanovsky Archive*

70 NOVEMBER 1974 *Richard Wright* auf der Bühne des Wembley Empire Pool in London (UK).
*Jill Furmanovsky Archive*

71 NOVEMBER 1973 *Nick Mason* beim Konzert im Londoner Rainbow Theatre.
*Jill Furmanovsky Archive*

72 APRIL 1975 Pink Floyd live im Pacific Coliseum, Vancouver (Kanada).
*Storm Thorgerson und Aubrey „Po" Powell, Hipgnosis, Pink Floyd Music Ltd*

73 MAI 1973 *Roger Waters* und der flammende Gong im Earls Court, London (UK).
*Jill Furmanovsky Archive*

74 NOVEMBER 1974 Pink-Floyd-Fans im Wembley Empire Pool in London, (UK).
*Storm Thorgerson und Aubrey „Po" Powell, Hipgnosis, Pink Floyd Music Ltd*

75 MAI 1973 *David Gilmour* beim Auftritt im Earls Court in London (UK).
*Jill Furmanovsky Archive*

76 NOVEMBER 1974 Die Band mit Projektionen auf der Bühnenleinwand im Empire Theatre, Liverpool (UK).
*Storm Thorgerson und Aubrey „Po" Powell, Hipgnosis, Pink Floyd Music Ltd*

77 NOVEMBER 1974 *David Gilmour, Nick Mason* und *Roger Waters* live mit Leinwandprojektionen im Empire Theatre, Liverpool (UK).
*Jill Furmanovsky Archive*

78 DEZEMBER 1974 *Nick Mason* und *Roger Waters* live mit Leinwandprojektionen im Palace Theatre, Manchester (UK).
*Jill Furmanovsky Archive*

79 DEZEMBER 1974 Projizierte Leinwandbilder von *Ian Emes* begleiten den Song „Time" im Palace Theatre in Manchester (UK).
*Jill Furmanovsky Archive*

80 APRIL 1975 Die Band live mit Leinwandprojektionen im Pacific Coliseum in Vancouver (Kanada).
*Storm Thorgerson und Aubrey „Po" Powell, Hipgnosis, Pink Floyd Music Ltd*

81 APRIL 1975 *Nick Mason* live im Pacific Coliseum in Vancouver (Kanada).
*Storm Thorgerson und Aubrey „Po“ Powell, Hipgnosis, Pink Floyd Music Ltd*

82 APRIL 1975 Die Begleitsängerinnen *Venetta Fields* und *Carlena Williams* in der Los Angeles Memorial Sports Arena (USA).
*Storm Thorgerson und Aubrey „Po“ Powell, Hipgnosis, Pink Floyd Music Ltd*

83 NOVEMBER 1974 *Roger Waters* auf der Bühne der Usher Hall, Edinburgh (UK).
*Jill Furmanovsky Archive*

84 NOVEMBER 1974 *David Gilmour* beim Konzert im Wembley Empire Pool, London (UK).
*Jill Furmanovsky Archive*

85 APRIL 1975 *Richard Wright* live im Pacific Coliseum in Vancouver (Kanada).
*Storm Thorgerson und Aubrey „Po“ Powell, Hipgnosis, Pink Floyd Music Ltd*

86 DEZEMBER 1974 Die Begleitsängerinnen *Venetta Fields* und *Carlena Williams* beim Auftritt im Palace Theatre, Manchester (UK).
*Jill Furmanovsky Archive*

87 NOVEMBER 1974 *Nick Mason* auf der Bühne des Wembley Empire Pool, London (UK).
*Jill Furmanovsky Archive*

88 NOVEMBER 1974 *Roger Waters* beim Auftritt im Wembley Empire Pool, London (UK).
*Jill Furmanovsky Archive*

89 APRIL 1975 Begleitsängerin *Carlena Williams* auf der Bühne der Los Angeles Memorial Sports Arena (USA).
*Storm Thorgerson und Aubrey „Po“ Powell, Hipgnosis, Pink Floyd Music Ltd*

90 DEZEMBER 1974 Pink-Floyd-Fans im Palace Theatre, Manchester (UK).
*Jill Furmanovsky Archive*

91 NOVEMBER 1974 Während die Band spielt, stürzt das Modellflugzeug auf die Bühne des Wembley Empire Pool, London (UK).
*Jill Furmanovsky Archive*

92 APRIL 1975 *Nick Mason* an seinem Ludwig-„Hokusai Wave“-Schlagzeug, handbemalt von *Kate Hepburn*, in der Los Angeles Memorial Sports Arena (USA).
*Storm Thorgerson und Aubrey „Po“ Powell, Hipgnosis, Pink Floyd Music Ltd*

93 APRIL 1975 *David Gilmour* mit seiner Lap-Steelgitarre in der Los Angeles Memorial Sports Arena (USA).
*Storm Thorgerson und Aubrey „Po“ Powell, Hipgnosis, Pink Floyd Music Ltd*

94 APRIL 1975 *David Gilmour* und *Richard Wright* beim Auftritt im Pacific Coliseum in Vancouver (Kanada).
*Storm Thorgerson und Aubrey „Po“ Powell, Hipgnosis, Pink Floyd Music Ltd*

95 APRIL 1975 *Roger Waters* und *Richard Wright* live in der Los Angeles Memorial Sports Arena (USA).
*Storm Thorgerson und Aubrey „Po“ Powell, Hipgnosis, Pink Floyd Music Ltd*

96 APRIL 1975 *Roger Waters* und *Richard Wright* live in der Los Angeles Memorial Sports Arena (USA).
*Storm Thorgerson und Aubrey „Po“ Powell, Hipgnosis, Pink Floyd Music Ltd*

97 APRIL 1975 *Roger Waters* und *Richard Wright* live im Pacific Coliseum, Vancouver (Kanada).
*Storm Thorgerson und Aubrey „Po“ Powell, Hipgnosis, Pink Floyd Music Ltd*

98 NOVEMBER 1974 Die Band, bestrahlt von Laser-Lichteffekten, im Wembley Empire Pool, London (GB).
*Jill Furmanovsky Archive*

99 NOVEMBER 1974 Pink-Floyd-Fans in der Usher Hall in Edinburgh (UK).
*Jill Furmanovsky Archive*

100 NOVEMBER 1974 *Nick Mason* beim Konzert in der Usher Hall, Edinburgh (UK).
*Jill Furmanovsky Archive*

101 APRIL 1975 *Roger Waters* auf der Bühne, Pacific Coliseum in Vancouver (Kanada).
*Storm Thorgerson und Aubrey „Po“ Powell, Hipgnosis, Pink Floyd Music Ltd*

102 JUNI 1972 *David Gilmour* beim Auftritt im Dome in Brighton (UK).
*Jill Furmanovsky Archive*

103 APRIL 1975 *Richard Wright* live im Tucson Community Center, Arizona (USA).
*Storm Thorgerson und Aubrey „Po“ Powell, Hipgnosis, Pink Floyd Music Ltd*

104 DEZEMBER 1974 *David Gilmour*, *Nick Mason* und *Roger Waters* beim Konzert im Palace Theatre, Manchester (UK).
*Jill Furmanovsky Archive*

105 DEZEMBER 1974 *Roger Waters* und Saxofonist *Dick Parry* beim Auftritt im Palace Theatre, Manchester (UK).
*Jill Furmanovsky Archive*

106 DEZEMBER 1974 *David Gilmour* auf der Bühne des Hippodrome, Birmingham (UK).
*Jill Furmanovsky Archive*

107 NOVEMBER 1974 *Roger Waters* beim Konzert in der Usher Hall, Edinburgh (UK).
*Jill Furmanovsky Archive*

108 DEZEMBER 1974 *Roger Waters* und *David Gilmour* live im Hippodrome, Birmingham (UK).
*Jill Furmanovsky Archive*

109 NOVEMBER 1974 *Richard Wright*, *Roger Waters*, *Nick Mason* und *David Gilmour* live im Wembley Empire Pool, London (UK).
*Storm Thorgerson und Aubrey „Po“ Powell, Hipgnosis, Pink Floyd Music Ltd*

110 NOVEMBER 1974 *Nick Mason* live im Wembley Empire Pool, London (UK).
*Jill Furmanovsky Archive*

111 APRIL 1975 *Richard Wright* beim Auftritt in der Los Angeles Memorial Sports Arena (USA).
*Storm Thorgerson und Aubrey „Po“ Powell, Hipgnosis, Pink Floyd Music Ltd*

112 NOVEMBER 1974 *David Gilmour* und die Begleitsängerinnen *Venetta Fields* und *Carlena Williams* mit Lichteffekten im Wembley Empire Pool, London (UK).
*Jill Furmanovsky Archive*

113 NOVEMBER 1974 Pink Floyd live im Empire Theatre, Liverpool (UK).
*Jill Furmanovsky Archive*

114 NOVEMBER 1974 Pink-Floyd-Fans im Wembley Empire Pool, London (UK).
*Jill Furmanovsky Archive*

115 NOVEMBER 1974 Leinwandprojektion auf der Bühne des Wembley Empire Pool, London (UK).
*Jill Furmanovsky Archive*

116 NOVEMBER 1974 *Roger Waters* auf der Bühne des Wembley Empire Pool, London (UK).
*Storm Thorgerson und Aubrey „Po“ Powell, Hipgnosis, Pink Floyd Music Ltd*

117 NOVEMBER 1974 Hände von Pink-Floyd-Fans, die eine Pyramide zeigen, im Wembley Empire Pool, London (UK).
*Storm Thorgerson und Aubrey „Po“ Powell, Hipgnosis, Pink Floyd Music Ltd*

118 APRIL 1975 Nach der Show in der Los Angeles Memorial Sports Arena (USA).
*Storm Thorgerson und Aubrey „Po“ Powell, Hipgnosis, Pink Floyd Music Ltd*

AFTER SHOW

120 DEZEMBER 1974 *Nick Mason*, *Roger Waters*, Begleitsängerin *Carlena Williams*, Gitarrencheftechniker *Phil Taylor* und andere Mitglieder der Crew in einer Bar, nach dem Konzert im Palace Theatre, Manchester (UK).
*Jill Furmanovsky Archive*

121 DEZEMBER 1974 *David Gilmour* mit den Begleitsängerinnen *Carlena Williams* und *Venetta Fields* in einer Bar, nach dem Auftritt im Palace Theatre, Manchester (UK).
*Jill Furmanovsky Archive*

122 DEZEMBER 1974 *David Gilmour*, *Roger Waters* und Hipgnosis-Designer *Storm Thorgerson* in einer Bar, nach dem Konzert im Palace Theatre, Manchester (UK).
*Jill Furmanovsky Archive*

123 DEZEMBER 1974 *Roger Waters* und Hipgnosis-Coverdesigner *Storm Thorgerson* in einer Bar, nach dem Auftritt im Palace Theatre, Manchester (UK).
*Jill Furmanovsky Archive*

124 APRIL 1975 *Richard Wright* an einem Skilift während des Aufenthalts der Band in Vancouver (Kanada).
*Storm Thorgerson und Aubrey „Po" Powell, Hipgnosis, Pink Floyd Music Ltd*

125 APRIL 1975 *David Gilmour* in einer Skihütte während des Abstechers nach Vancouver (Kanada).
*Storm Thorgerson und Aubrey „Po" Powell, Hipgnosis, Pink Floyd Music Ltd*

126 DEZEMBER 1974 *Nick Mason* und *Richard Wright* in einem Sportclub während der Tourdates im Hippodrome, Birmingham (UK).
*Jill Furmanovsky Archive*

127 DEZEMBER 1974 In einem Sportclub lesen *David Gilmour* und *Richard Wright* die *Sun* und den *Daily Mirror* (Schlagzeile: „Wilsons Pläne für die Marktwirtschaft"), während der Tourdates im Hippodrome, Birmingham (UK).
*Jill Furmanovsky Archive*

128 DEZEMBER 1974 *Roger Waters* und Bandkumpel *Nick Sedgwick* beim Golfen während der Tourdates im Palace Theatre, Manchester (UK).
*Jill Furmanovsky Archive*

129 DEZEMBER 1974 *Roger Waters*, *David Gilmour* und Hipgnosis-Grafiker *Storm Thorgerson* beim Squash in einem Sportclub während der Dates im Hippodrome, Birmingham (UK).
*Storm Thorgerson und Aubrey „Po" Powell, Hipgnosis, Pink Floyd Music Ltd*

130 DEZEMBER 1974 *Roger Waters* beim Squashspielen während der Tourdates im Hippodrome, Birmingham (UK).
*Storm Thorgerson und Aubrey „Po" Powell, Hipgnosis, Pink Floyd Music Ltd*

131 NOVEMBER 1974 *Richard Wright* in einem Sportclub beim Squash während der Tourdates in der Usher Hall, Edinburgh (UK).
*Jill Furmanovsky Archive*

132 NOVEMBER 1974 *David Gilmour* spielt Squash in einem Sportclub während der Tourdates in der Usher Hall in Edinburgh (UK).
*Jill Furmanovsky Archive*

133 NOVEMBER 1974 *David Gilmour* und *Nick Mason* beim Squashspielen in einem Sportclub während der Tourdates in der Usher Hall, Edinburgh (UK).
*Jill Furmanovsky Archive*

134 DEZEMBER 1974 *Nick Mason* im Speisewagen des Intercity nach Birmingham während der Wintertournee durch Großbritannien.
*Jill Furmanovsky Archive*

135 DEZEMBER 1974 *Roger Waters*, Toningenieur *Brian Humphries* und Tourmanager *Warwick McCredie* im Intercity nach Birmingham während der Wintertournee durch Großbritannien.
*Jill Furmanovsky Archive*

136 DEZEMBER 1974 Rockfotografin *Jill Furmanovsky* im Intercity nach Birmingham während der Wintertournee durch Großbritannien.
*Jill Furmanovsky Archive*

137 DEZEMBER 1974 *Roger Waters* und *Nick Mason* im Intercity nach Birmingham während der Wintertournee durch Großbritannien.
*Jill Furmanovsky Archive*

138 NOVEMBER 1974 *David Gilmour*, Rockfotografin *Jill Furmanovsky* und Pink-Floyd-Freund *Nick Sedgwick* im Intercity nach Birmingham während der Wintertournee durch Großbritannien.
*Storm Thorgerson und Aubrey „Po" Powell, Hipgnosis, Pink Floyd Music Ltd*

139 NOVEMBER 1974 *David Gilmour*, Tourmanager *Warwick McCredie*, Begleitsängerin *Carlena Williams*, Saxofonist *Dick Parry* und Hipgnosis-Designer *Storm Thorgerson* (mit Kamera) beim Einchecken im Hotel vor dem Auftritt in der Usher Hall, Edinburgh (UK).
*Jill Furmanovsky Archive*

140 NOVEMBER 1974 *David Gilmour*, *Richard Wright* und Hipgnosis-Designer *Storm Thorgerson* beim Backgammonspiel im Hotelzimmer in Edinburgh (UK).
*Jill Furmanovsky Archive*

141 NOVEMBER 1974 *David Gilmour*, *Richard Wright* und die Hipgnosis-Albumdesigner *Aubrey „Po" Powell* und *Storm Thorgerson* während der Wintertournee durch Großbritannien.
*Jill Furmanovsky Archive*

ARTWORKS

143 VINYL-LABEL 1973
*Hipgnosis / George Hardie*

144–145 KLEBEMUSTER FÜR FRONT- & BACKCOVER 1973
*Hipgnosis / George Hardie*

146–147 FRONT- & BACKCOVER 1973
*Hipgnosis / George Hardie*

148–149 KLEBEMUSTER FÜR INNENKLAPPE 1973
*Hipgnosis / George Hardie*

150–151 INNENKLAPPE 1973
*Hipgnosis / George Hardie*

152–153 PYRAMIDEN-PLAKAT 1973
*Hipgnosis*

158 PINK FLOYD 1971 *Richard Wright*, *Nick Mason*, *Roger Waters* und *David Gilmour* im Belsize Park, London (UK).
*Pink Floyd Music Ltd*

159 PINK FLOYD 1971 *Richard Wright*, *Nick Mason*, *Roger Waters* und *David Gilmour* verbergen ihre Gesichter im Belsize Park, London (UK).
*Pink Floyd Music Ltd*

160 JANUAR 1972 Doppelseitige Anzeige im *Melody Maker* mit den Pink-Floyd-Tourdaten für die ersten zwei Monate des Jahres.
*Pink Floyd Archive*

---

Erstveröffentlichung in Großbritannien 2023
Thames & Hudson Ltd, 181A High Holborn, London WC1V 7QX

Erstveröffentlichung in den USA 2023
Thames & Hudson Inc. 500 Fifth Avenue, New York, New York, 10110

Erstveröffentlichung in Deutschland 2023
Edel Books, Neumühlen 17, 22763 Hamburg



Kuratiert von JILL FURMANOVSKY

Artdirector AUBREY POWELL

Design: Pentagram 2022

Bildkommentare: Tracey Kraft, Pink Floyd Stills Archivist



ISBN 978-3-8419-0844-5

Printed and bound in Italy by Printer Trento s.r.l.

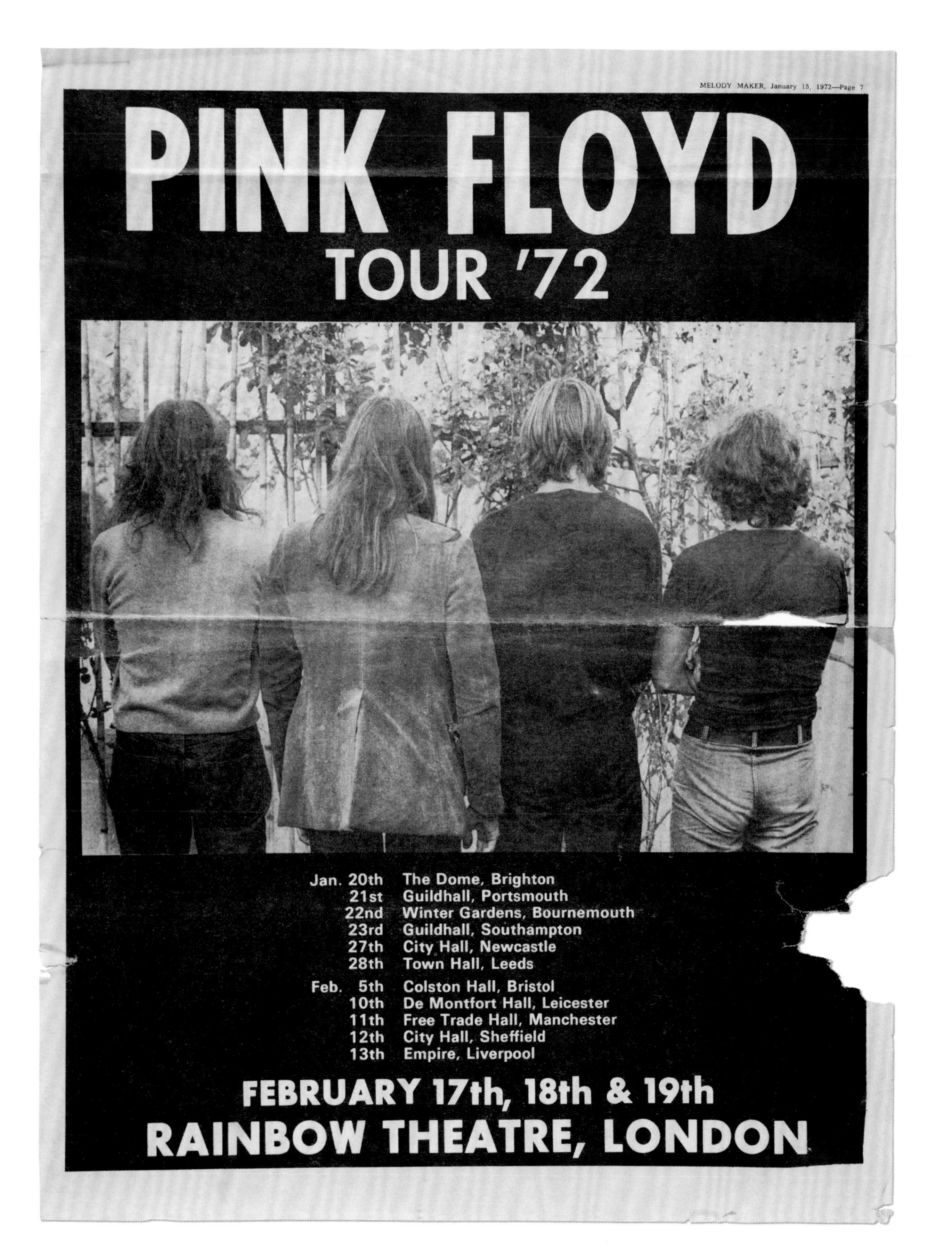
MELODY MAKER, January 15, 1972—Page 7
PINK FLOYD
TOUR '72
Jan. 20th The Dome, Brighton
21st Guildhall, Portsmouth
22nd Winter Gardens, Bournemouth
23rd Guildhall, Southampton
27th City Hall, Newcastle
28th Town Hall, Leeds
Feb. 5th Colston Hall, Bristol
10th De Montfort Hall, Leicester
11th Free Trade Hall, Manchester
12th City Hall, Sheffield
13th Empire, Liverpool
FEBRUARY 17th, 18th & 19th
RAINBOW THEATRE, LONDON